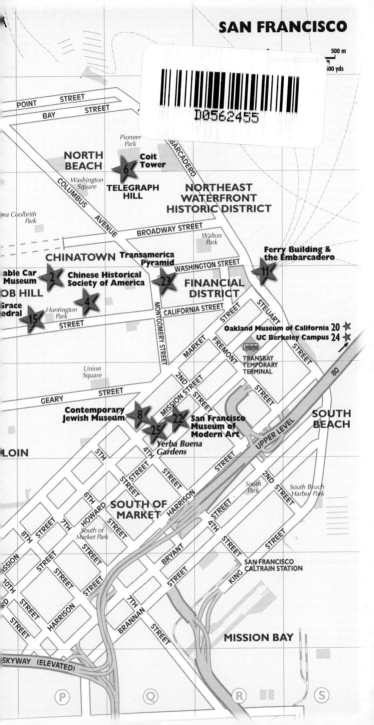

SAN FRANCISCO

500 m
500 yds

NORTH BEACH

Pioneer Park

6 **Coit Tower**

Washington Square

TELEGRAPH HILL

NORTHEAST WATERFRONT HISTORIC DISTRICT

na Coolbrith Park

BROADWAY STREET

Walton Park

CHINATOWN **Transamerica Pyramid**

WASHINGTON STREET

Ferry Building & the Embarcadero

11

able Car Museum **2** **Chinese Historical Society of America** **23**

FINANCIAL DISTRICT

OB HILL

race edral **15** Huntington Park **4**

CALIFORNIA STREET

STREET

Oakland Museum of California 20

UC Berkeley Campus 24

Union Square

TRANSBAY TEMPORARY TERMINAL

80

GEARY STREET

Contemporary Jewish Museum **8** **22** **San Francisco Museum of Modern Art**

LOIN

25 **Yerba Buena Gardens**

SOUTH BEACH

South Park

South Beach Harbor Park

SOUTH OF MARKET

South of Market Park

MISSION BAY

SAN FRANCISCO CALTRAIN STATION

SKYWAY (ELEVATED)

(P)   (Q)   (R)   (S)

Fodor's
25BEST
San Francisco

by Mick Sinclair

Fodor's Travel Publications
New York • Toronto • London • Sydney • Auckland
www.fodors.com

Contents

KEY TO SYMBOLS

➕ Map reference to the accompanying pull-out map

✉ Address

☎ Telephone number

🕐 Opening/closing times

🍴 Restaurant or café

🚆 Nearest rail station

Ⓜ Nearest subway (BART) station

🚌 Nearest bus route

ENTERTAINMENT 128

Whether you're after a cultural fix or just want a place to relax with a drink after a hard day's sight-seeing, we've made the best choices for you.

EAT 138

Uncover great dining experiences, from a quick bite at lunch to top-notch evening meals.

SLEEP 150

We've brought together the best hotels in the city, whatever budget you're on.

NEED TO KNOW 160

The practical information you need to make your trip run smoothly.

PULL-OUT MAP

The pull-out map accompanying this book is a comprehensive street plan of the city. We've given grid references within the book for each sight and listing.

🖻 Nearest riverboat or ferry stop	🎟 Admission charges:
♿ Facilities for visitors with disabilities	Expensive (over \$13), Moderate (\$7–\$13) and
🔢 Tourist information	Inexpensive (under \$7)
❓ Other practical information	▷ Further information

Introducing San Francisco

Since the Gold Rush transformed San Francisco from a hamlet into a city in the 1850s, it has been different from other cities. An anything-goes atmosphere of the early days forged a lasting mood of tolerance and a welcoming attitude toward change.

Home to a multitude of races, religions and cultures, San Francisco is intensely cosmopolitan. The diverse population has fueled the personality of the city and its multicultural draws: the varied dining scene, museums and galleries celebrating the experiences and contributions of Asians, Africans, Jews and many other groups; and neighborhoods like Chinatown and the Latino Mission District that show the vitality of these communities today.

San Francisco has frequently set the nation's cultural and social pace, and it continues to do so. It witnessed the birth of the 1950s Beat generation, of the hippie era in the 1960s, and of the gay and lesbian liberation movement in the 1970s. Through the 1990s, its multimedia and internet companies set the pace for the global information revolution. Today, companies like Google, Facebook and Apple are ensuring that the area continues to lead the charge in the next wave of technological advances. On environmental issues, San Francisco is leading the charge as well. Its 2007 ban on plastic bags at grocery stores and pharmacies reduced plastic bag use by five million per month.

Despite its importance on the national and international stage, San Francisco is small by big-city standards, housing about 815,000 people on a peninsula that is not only scenically spectacular but also prevents sprawl. The area divides into neighborhoods linked by public transportation and many are easy to walk between and through, and are well within reach of downtown, the business hub, and tourist-heavy Fisherman's Wharf.

It's easy to understand why this city is the most visited in the US. As the *San Francisco Chronicle* columnist Herb Caen once said, "One day if I do go to heaven, I'll look around and say, 'It ain't bad, but it ain't San Francisco.'"

FACTS AND FIGURES

- In the event of another Bay Area earthquake like the ones in 1906 and 1989, the Golden Gate Bridge is designed to sway 27.7ft (8.4m).
- San Francisco's steepest streets, Filbert and 22nd streets, have a 31.5 percent gradient.
- The only National Historic Landmarks that travel are the city's iconic cable cars.

WHAT'S IN A NAME

In 1835 San Francisco was a growing settlement called Yerba Buena (Spanish for "good herb"), but after the United States laid claim to California during the Mexican-American War, the territory was renamed San Francisco. The start of the Gold Rush followed in 1848 and 1849, transforming the city and giving a future football team its name.

CAUGHT ON FILM

Scenic hills and views make the city an enticing place as a backdrop for films (▷ 171). Classic movies filmed here include *Vertigo* (1958), *The Maltese Falcon* (1941), *The Caine Mutiny* (1954) and *The Graduate* (1967). More recently, *The Pursuit of Happyness* (2006) and *The Rock* (1996) were shot in San Francisco.

EMPEROR NORTON

Wearing epaulettes and a cockaded hat, eccentric businessman Joshua Norton proclaimed himself "Emperor of the United States and Protector of Mexico" in 1856. He was effectively accepted as such in San Francisco, though his antics were dismissed by the US government. On his death in 1880, the city's flags flew at half-mast.

Focus On Outdoor Activities

There's a reason San Francisco is ranked among the top 10 fittest cities in the US in a report published by the American College of Sports Medicine. Folks in this town get up early to run, bike and swim—not to mention playing golf, tennis and other sports. The area is also blessed with unique outdoor fitness options, including urban stairway walks, stunning Marin trails and free tennis courts.

Hiking and Bicycling

San Francisco and Marin County may be the Holy Grail for hiking and bicycling enthusiasts. The flat path along the Marina Green and Crissy Field (▷ 39) is popular with bicyclists, runners and casual walkers. Many bicyclists then ride across the Golden Gate Bridge and continue into Marin—views from the Coastal/Matt Davis trail in Mount Tamalpais State Park are incredible. Golden Gate Park (▷ 40–41), Angel Island (▷ 75) and many swaths of the Golden Gate National Recreation Area (▷ 38–39) also offer excellent trails to accommodate various fitness levels. Bicycle rental shops are easy to find, especially near Fisherman's Wharf.

Stairway Walks

You don't need to leave the city to hike. With more than 40 hills and 300 stairways, San Francisco offers urban hikes for the energetic traveler. The stairs are usually made of concrete in urban areas and wood elsewhere. Memorable stairway walks include the Filbert Steps, which start near Coit Tower and end in Levi Plaza; the Lyon Stairs, popular with boot camps on weekday mornings (Lyon between Broadway and Green); and scenic Land's End, part of the Golden Gate National Recreation Area (visit www.parksconservancy.org/visit/park-sites/lands-end.html for additional information). The famous Dipsea Race in Mill Valley (in Marin) includes stairs.

Clockwise from top: Windsurfers in front of the Golden Gate Bridge; climbing the Filbert Steps, near Coit Tower; San Francisco has more than 150 public tennis courts;

Water Sports

Intrepid surfers brave the chilly waters of Ocean Beach, a popular Bay Area surfing spot. Wearing a wetsuit is a must, and take precautions—this beach is known for strong currents. To rent a wetsuit or surfboard near Ocean Beach, try Aqua Surf Shop (2830 Sloat Boulevard; tel 415/242–9283). In Golden Gate Park, visit Stow Lake Bike & Boat Rentals (50 Stow Lake Drive; tel 415/752–0347) to rent four-person rowboats or paddleboats. Across the Golden Gate Bridge in Sausalito, Sea Trek Sausalito (▷ 77) is the place to go for kayak rentals and guided trips on the water. The Bay Area also has a number of harbors and plenty of sailing and windsurfing opportunities.

Golf and Tennis

While the majority of the state's 1,000 or more golf courses are in Southern California, the Bay Area has its fair share. Popular public courses include the Presidio Golf Course (tel 415/561–GOLF; www.presidiogolf.com) and Lincoln Park Golf Club (tel 415/221–9911; www.lincolnparkgc.com). San Francisco also has more than 150 public tennis courts, around 130 of which can be used free of charge (visit www.sftenniscourts.com).

Spectator Sports

Professional sports teams in the Bay Area include the San Francisco Giants (tel 415/972–2000; http://sanfrancisco.giants.mlb.com) and the East Bay's Oakland A's (tel 510/638–4627; http://oakland.athletics.mlb.com), both part of Major League Baseball; Oakland's Golden State Warriors (tel 510/986–2200; www.nba.com/warriors), part of the National Basketball Association; and two teams from the National Football League—the Oakland Raiders (tel 510/864–5000; www.raiders.com) and the San Francisco 49ers (tel 415/656–4900; www.49ers.com).

fans cheer their heroes at the San Francisco Giants victory parade, in 2010; a bicyclist in Marin County admires the Golden Gate Bridge; surfing the waves

Top Tips For...

These great suggestions will help you tailor your ideal visit to San Francisco, no matter how you choose to spend your time.

...Late-Night Dining
Eat in the Western Addition at **NoPa** (▷ 147) or **Tsunami** (▷ 149).
Brave the gritty Tenderloin for Indian fare at **Shalimar** (▷ 148).
Nibble on small plates at **Alembic** (▷ 132) in the Upper Haight.

...Learning About Different Cultures
Take a tour of the **Mission District Murals** (▷ 71–72).
Learn about the African diaspora at **MoAD** (▷ 72).
Walk around the neighborhoods of **Japantown** (▷ 46–47) and **Chinatown** (▷ 67).
Visit the **Contemporary Jewish Museum** (▷ 28–29).

...Vintage or Funky Finds
Pay a visit to **Ver Unica** (▷ 126–127) in Hayes Valley.
Peruse Haight Street in **Haight-Ashbury** (▷ 70, 121) for the best wacky, vintage clothes outlets.
Discover secondhand designer clothes at **Cris** (▷ 123).
Head over to the **Mission District** (▷ 71–72, 121) to shop, where you will find a range of funky designs.

...Outdoor Activities
Boat across Stow Lake in **Golden Gate Park** (▷ 40–41).
Bike to **Sausalito** (▷ 77) via the **Golden Gate Bridge** (▷ 36–37).
Hike around **Angel Island** (▷ 75).
Surf at Ocean Beach in the **Golden Gate National Recreation Area** (▷ 38–39).

Clockwise from top left: Colorful clothes for sale in Haight-Ashbury; walking across the Golden Gate Bridge; enjoying the view at Greens restaurant; Cobb's is a

...Saving Money

Ride to the top of the observation tower (free entry) at the **de Young Museum** (▷ 30–31).
Walk along the pedestrian path of the **Golden Gate Bridge** (▷ 36–37).
Enjoy a burrito at **Taqueria Cancun** in the **Mission** (▷ 149).
Get in free at the city's cathedrals, **Grace** (▷ 42–43) and **St. Mary's** (▷ 73).

...Entertaining Your Children

Jump on a **cable car** (▷ 167) for a slow-moving adventure.
Visit the Tactile Dome at the **Exploratorium** (▷ 32–33).
Meet the animals at the **San Francisco Zoo** (▷ 75).
Take the ferry over to **Alcatraz** for a fun history lesson (▷ 14–15).

...Dining with a View

Enjoy vegetarian food and bay views at **Greens** (▷ 144–145).
Admire the Bay Bridge while dining at **Boulevard** (▷ 143).
Watch the cable car chug by at **Zarzuela** (▷ 149).
Have a pisco sour and ceviche along the **Embarcadero** (▷ 34–35).

...Hearty Laughs

See an improv show at **BATS** (▷ 133), in Fort Mason.
Check out the stand-up comedians at **Punch Line** comedy club (▷ 136).
See who's topping the bill at **Cobb's** (▷ 134).
View an exhibition at the **Cartoon Art Museum** (▷ 66–67).

...Specialty Books and Magazines

Learn about the Beat at **City Lights** (▷ 123).
Find indie magazines at **Needles & Pens** (▷ 126).

great place for comedy; books line the shelves at City Lights; boating on Stow Lake, in Golden Gate Park

Timeline

1769 The Spanish discover San Francisco Bay.

1821 Mexico takes California from Spain.

1846 The United States takes control of California by force from Mexico.

1848–49 The California Gold Rush begins. San Francisco's population soars from only 812 to 20,000 as the city becomes the commercial center for miners.

GAY PROTEST

In 1977 Harvey Milk became the nation's first openly gay male to be elected to public office. The following year, Milk and Mayor George Moscone were assassinated at City Hall by a former city politician, Dan White. The lightweight five-year prison sentence bestowed on White prompted the White Night Riots; predominantly gay demonstrators marched on City Hall, causing $1 million dollars worth of damage. The 2008 film *Milk* tells Harvey Milk's story (▷ 171).

1873 The first cable car runs along Clay Street.

1906 San Francisco is ruined by earthquake and fire.

1915 The Panama Pacific International Exposition symbolizes the city's recovery from the earthquake.

1937 The Golden Gate Bridge is completed.

1941 US entry into World War II stimulates war industries and brings an influx of military and civilian personnel to the city. Employment in the shipyards increases from 4,000 to 260,000.

1945 50 countries sign the United Nations charter in the SF Opera House.

1964 Students at Berkeley form the non-violent Free Speech Movement and instigate the first of many campus revolts in the country.

A cable car in the 1880s

A vast crack in one of the city's roads, caused by the 1906 earthquake

THE GREAT EARTHQUAKE

Striking at 5.12am on April 18, 1906, the earthquake measured 7.9 on the Richter scale but caused relatively minor damage. By rupturing gas and water mains, however, it caused fires to break out and burn uncontrolled for three days. Over 3,000 acres (1,215ha) of San Francisco had been devastated, 250,000 of the city's 400,000 inhabitants had been made homeless and 300 were dead (later reports suggest as many as 3,000 perished). The quake was a forceful reminder of the area's geological instability; the recovery highlighted San Francisco's regenerative powers, symbolized by the city's official emblem, the phoenix.

1966 The militant African-American group the Black Panthers forms in Oakland.

1967 The "Summer of Love": Young people arrive from across the US and Haight-Ashbury's hippie population grows to 75,000.

1989 The Loma Prieta earthquake (7.1 on the Richter scale) kills 67 people and closes the Bay Bridge for a month.

1995 Willie Brown becomes the city's first black mayor.

1996 San Francisco becomes the first local government to sue the tobacco industry.

1998 It becomes illegal to smoke in public indoor spaces.

1999 The $3.3 billion injected into San Francisco-based dotcom companies reshapes the city's economic base.

2002 A continuing decline of the dotcom economy brings financial uncertainty.

2004 Much publicized same-sex weddings take place at City Hall as 1,600 gay couples apply for licenses.

2007 San Francisco Representative Nancy Pelosi becomes the first female—and the first Californian—Speaker of the US House of Representatives.

2010 San Francisco's Major League Baseball team, the Giants, wins the World Series for the first time since moving from New York City in 1958.

"BEATNIKS"

The 1957 publication of Allen Ginsberg's poem *Howl* by North Beach bookstore-publisher City Lights (▷ 123) made the area a prime destination for what long-time *San Francisco Chronicle* columnist Herb Caen labeled "beatniks."

A Haight-Ashbury mural

Top 25

This section contains the must-see Top 25 sights and experiences in San Francisco. They are listed alphabetically, and numbered so you can locate them on the inside front cover map.

DID YOU KNOW?

● Named: Isla de los Alcatraces (Island of Pelicans), 1775
● Island size: 22.5 acres (9ha)
● Number of prisoners: 1,545
● Number of cells: 378

TIPS

● There is no food service on the island, so consider a snack on the ferry ride over.
● The evening tour is more expensive than the day tours.

Easily viewed from any high point in the city, Alcatraz is as much a part of San Francisco as the Golden Gate Bridge or cable cars. The former prison sits on Alcatraz Island in San Francisco Bay and is the city's most chilling sight.

No escape Alcatraz became the country's most feared place of incarceration from 1934, after the federal government took control of the island. It was turned into a top-security penitentiary for "incorrigible" criminals (those deemed beyond salvation and considered too dangerous to be held at conventional jails). There was one guard for every three inmates, work was a privilege that had to be earned through good behavior, and prisoners who did escape faced the prospect of crossing the freezing, swiftly

Alcatraz was a grim place of incarceration from 1934 until 1963; today visitors can tour the former prison and get a glimpse of what life was like for the inmates

moving waters of the bay (regarded as unswimmable) to freedom. Known escape attempts number 36 inmates in 14 separate attempts; five escapees are unaccounted for.

Moody viewing The former cells, mess hall, hospital and exercise yard are all open for viewing, and an audio tour with a terse commentary by former Alcatraz guards and inmates makes an excellent atmospheric accompaniment. The costs and difficulties of running an island prison, and public disquiet at the severity of the regime, contributed to Alcatraz's closure in 1963. A small museum traces the broader history of the island, which was claimed and occupied by Native Americans in 1969 for 19 months under an 1868 treaty that granted them rights to "unused government land."

THE BASICS

www.nps.gov/alcatraz
➕ Off map at N1
✉ San Francisco Bay
☎ 415/981–7625
🕐 Daily, according to first and last ferries
⛴ Alcatraz Cruises from Pier 33, Fisherman's Wharf
♿ Few
💰 Expensive. Advance reservations advised in summer; buy tickets online at www.alcatrazcruises.com

DID YOU KNOW?

- First cable car run: August 2, 1873
- First route: Clay Street
- Most cars in use: 600
- Most miles of track: 110 (177km)
- Current number of cars in use: 40
- Current miles of track: 11 (18km)
- Width of cable: 1.25in (3.5cm)
- Average speed of cable car: 9.5mph (15.5kph)
- Annual cable car passengers: 10.5 million

The ring of the cable-car bell provides a constant reminder that you are in San Francisco, probably the only city in the world where a relatively inefficient form of public transportation is adored by the entire population.

Inspired Legend has it that a horse, slipping while trying to drag its load up a San Franciscan hill, inspired Andrew Smith Hallidie to invent the cable car. Wire rope had previously been used as a means of transporting materials in gold mines, but Hallidie was the first to develop the idea as a means of moving people. Damage caused by the 1906 earthquake and fire, and the subsequent rise of motorized transportation, soon rendered cable cars obsolete. Pressure from San Franciscans led the

Find out how this much-loved form of city transportation works at the Cable Car Museum

federal government to award National Historic Landmark status to cable cars in 1964, however, and a provision in the city's charter ensures preservation of the remaining lines.

Simple but effective The museum's intriguing memorabilia, including the first cable car, tell the story of the system's development. The clever engineering principle that keeps the cars running is also revealed: Each one is pulled by an underground cable that never stops moving. The "gripman" on each car uses a lever to connect or disconnect the car to or from the cable through a slot in the road. The whirring sound, audible as you enter the museum, is the noise made by the steel cable as it is pulled over winding wheels that are 14ft (4.5m) wide, a process visible in the museum's lower level.

THE BASICS

www.cablecarmuseum.org

➕ P4

✉ 1201 Mason Street

☎ 415/474–1887

🕐 Apr–Sep daily 10–6; Oct–Mar 10–5

🚃 1, 3, 12, 45; Powell–Mason or Powell–Hyde cable car

♿ Good

🎟 Free

3 California Academy of Sciences

After a significant renovation, the California Academy of Sciences returned to Golden Gate Park with a splash in 2008. The "green" museum shelters a rainforest dome, planetarium, aquarium and natural history museum under its living roof. The building, designed by Renzo Piano, has gained the highest LEED sustainability rating.

The sky The all-digital, state-of-the-art Morrison Planetarium is the biggest draw at the museum. Popular shows about the stars and planets happen every half hour during the week, and every 45 minutes on weekends. There is no extra cost, but visitors need a separate ticket, which is handed out on a first-come, first-served basis. It's advisable to get your tickets before you start exploring the museum.

A rainforest, planetarium and aquarium are among the attractions at the California Academy of Sciences

Land and sea Near the Planetarium on the main floor is the Kimball Natural History Museum and the hall of dioramas. The exhibits cover topics like evolution on remote islands, how climate change is affecting California's natural habitat and the diverse ecosystems of Africa. You can also peek through windows to see Academy scientists doing their research. Downstairs is the Steinhart Aquarium, with 38,000 live animals across 900 species. Be warned that the space can feel a bit cramped.

The forest The museum also has a rainforest—within a glass dome—that houses an array of tropical plants and 1,600 animals, from a cave of bats to reptiles and butterflies. The temperature here is 82°F to 85°F (28°C to 29°C), plus 75 percent humidity.

THE BASICS

www.calacademy.org

➕ G7

✉ 55 Concourse Drive, Golden Gate Park

☎ 415/379–8000

🕐 Mon–Sat 9.30–5, Sun 11–5

🚍 5, 44, N–Judah

♿ Good

💵 Expensive

DID YOU KNOW?

● Proportion of factory jobs held by Chinese in San Francisco in 1872: 50 percent

● Chinese in San Francisco in 1875: 35,000

● Chinese in San Francisco in 1882: 26,000

● Chinese in San Francisco in 1900: 14,000

● Chinese arrivals to San Francisco, 1910–40: 175,000

● Estimated number of Chinese-Americans in San Francisco in 2000: 150,000

The Chinese have been present for longer, and in much greater numbers, than any other non-Anglo ethnic group in San Francisco, greatly contributing to the city's multicultural character.

Early days The Chinese arrived in California in force during the Gold Rush, but met racial hostility and the foreign miners' tax. They were unjustly blamed for the economic depression that followed the gold boom and were eventually forced into "Chinatown" communities, the largest being in San Francisco. Chinatown became populated almost exclusively by males who wore traditional dress and tied their hair in braids. Developing into the city's most densely populated district, Chinatown was composed of wooden buildings divided by slender alleyways

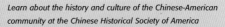
Learn about the history and culture of the Chinese-American community at the Chinese Historical Society of America

where, denied the comforts of traditional family life, many Chinese men gambled, smoked opium, joined the secret Chinese-American societies known as tongs and visited prostitutes to alleviate the boredom—activities that added to the area's mystique.

Recent times Not until the founding of the Chinese Republic in 1911 were the Chinese able to adopt Western ideas and modes of dress. By the 1920s, Chinatown's restaurants and shops were becoming tourist attractions and the Chinese, expanded in numbers through the easing of immigration restrictions, steadily became an accepted part of life. This tiny museum tells the story of the Chinese in California, with exhibits ranging from an antique silver pagoda to gold-mining paraphernalia.

THE BASICS

www.chsa.org

✚ P4

✉ 965 Clay Street

☎ 415/391–1188

🕐 Tue–Fri 12–5, Sat 12–4

🚌 1, 30; Powell–Hyde cable car

♿ Few

🎟 Inexpensive; free 1st Thu of month

DID YOU KNOW?

● Architects: Brown and Bakewell

● Building cost: $3.5 million

● Year completed: 1915

● Occupants: mayor, elected for four-year term, and Board of Supervisors, the 11-member city legislature

● Assassination: Mayor George Moscone and Supervisor Harvey Milk, 1978

● Weddings: many, including in 1980 that of Mayor Dianne Feinstein, who invited the entire city

The crowning glory of the Civic Center, City Hall is a beaux-arts masterpiece with a dome that can be seen from many points around San Francisco. The esthetic appeal makes it seem an entirely fitting place for San Francisco to conduct its day-to-day administrative affairs.

A symbol City Hall's immense rotunda is topped by a black-and-gold copper dome (possibly modeled on St. Peter's, in Rome) visible across much of the city. This intricate and inspiring building at the heart of San Francisco was completed in 1915, and arose from the drawing boards of architects Arthur Brown and John Bakewell (both architects studied at the École des Beaux-Arts in Paris). In San Francisco, the authorities were eager for a building to

City Hall was commissioned to show San Francisco's superiority over rival Los Angeles; its architects used the French baroque style to great effect

symbolize San Francisco's superiority over fast-growing Los Angeles. It was Brown and Bakewell's plan—based on the French baroque style, making free use of marble and with hardly a square inch left bare of some form of decoration—that won the day.

Impressive interior Go inside and climb the grand staircase, which is lined by ornate wrought-iron banisters and illuminated by freestanding and hanging lamps, and wander around the landings where porticoes and arches, topped by neoclassical sculptured guardians, give access to the upper levels. With the removal of the county courts, the building gained space as well as strength after a four-year, $300-million structural refit completed in 1999.

THE BASICS

www.sfgsa.org (then enter keyword "City Hall")

☐ N6

✉ 1 Dr. Carlton B. Goodlett Place

☎ 415/554–4000

🕐 Mon–Fri 8–8

🚇 Civic Center or Van Ness

🚌 5, 10, 21, 47, 49

♿ Good

💲 Free

❓ Tours: Mon–Fri 10, 12, 2

HIGHLIGHTS

- Stunning views
- 19 frescoed murals
- Observation gallery

TIPS

- Parking is available but extremely limited (about 30 spots). To avoid getting stuck in a traffic jam, opt for a bit of exercise and walk up Filbert to Coit Tower.
- The continuation of Filbert is a set of charming wooden steps that lead down to Levi Plaza.

Whether from the top of the tower or from its base, the view across San Francisco Bay and a huge swath of the city is memorable, as are the murals—part of a Depression-era project to give work to artists.

History Coit Tower was built as a monument to Lillie Hitchcock Coit, a San Francisco socialite who was passionate about the fire department —she was cremated wearing a gold pin from Engine Company Number Five—and the city. She bequeathed $125,000 to San Francisco "for the purpose of adding beauty to the city which I have always loved." Construction began soon after her death in 1929, and the tower was completed in 1933 (the surrounding summit of Telegraph Hill, called Pioneer Park, was donated to the city in 1876).

Clockwise from far left: Coit Tower at dusk, with Oakland Bridge behind it; a statue of Christopher Columbus stands nearby; artists decorated the tower's walls with murals, including the orchard scene California, *by Maxine Albro; another mural—*Industries of California, *by Ralph Stackpole*

Frescoed murals In the early 1930s, artists were paid $38 per week to work on frescoed murals, which cover the bare walls of the tower. They were painted in the social realist style pioneered by Diego Rivera. The style was controversial, but only one fresco was censored: The phrase "Workers of the World Unite" appeared above the depiction of a surveyor and steel worker, along with other symbols and statements. That section was covered over.

The tower This fluted concrete column has a small observation gallery at the top, accessible by elevator. Reaching a height of 180ft (55m), the monument is visible from many areas of the city. Official Coit Tower literature refutes the rumor that the tower was built to look like a firehouse nozzle.

THE BASICS

➕ Q2 and Q3
✉ Summit of Telegraph Hill Boulevard
☎ 415/362–0808
🕐 Daily 10–6.30
🚌 39
♿ Few
💵 Inexpensive
❓ Guided tours of the murals Wed, Sat 11am

DID YOU KNOW?

- Architect: Bernard Cahill
- Year completed: 1898
- Original owners: Oddfellows Cemetery
- Number of niches: approximately 20,000
- Number of unoccupied niches: 30
- Most expensive currently available niche: $72,000
- Least expensive currently available niche: $14,000
- Most unusual niche adornment: W. C. Field's brandy decanter. There is also a niche with Elvis heads!

One way to convince San Franciscans you know more about their city than they do is to tell them about the Columbarium, one of the city's most architecturally noteworthy buildings, but one that most locals are unaware of.

The moving dead An elegant, four-story Victorian rotunda decorated with stained glass, the Columbarium (a final resting place for urns holding the ashes of the deceased) was designed by British architect Bernard Cahill and opened in 1898. By 1937, it stood in the heart of a 3-acre (1.5ha) cemetery in which an estimated 10,000 people were buried. That year, however, concerns for public health resulted in cemeteries being declared illegal in San Francisco; the graves (except for those at

The Columbarium opened in 1898; its niches hold urns containing the ashes of the deceased

Mission Dolores and the Presidio) were exhumed and their contents moved out of the city.

Notable niches Declared a memorial, the Columbarium itself was spared demolition but, with cremations being outlawed, it was left to decay. Restoration of the handsome structure began in 1980, and its empty niches were once again put on sale. Guided tours of the site focus on the architecture, but even a swift glance at the niches reveals Eddys, Turks and other once-illustrious families who gave their names to streets in the city. The Columbarium also has a memorial to gay-rights activist Harvey Milk, an American politician and the first openly gay city supervisor, who was assassinated in 1978 (▷ 10).

THE BASICS

✚ H6

✉ 1 Loraine Court (near Anza Street)

☎ 415/752–7891

🕐 Mon–Fri 9–5, Sat–Sun 10–3

🚌 33, 38

♿ None

💲 Free

❓ Call to arrange a tour

8 Contemporary Jewish Museum

Famed architect Daniel Libeskind designed the Contemporary Jewish Museum, redeveloping the 1907 landmark Jessie Street Power Substation. The ambitious, 63,000sq ft (5,853sq m) building extends the original Willis Polk-designed space, juxtaposing early 20th-century architecture with contemporary design.

Old and new Libeskind created a striking exterior for the museum's new home (it moved to its SoMa quarters in 2008), preserving something old and introducing something entirely modern and new. At first glance the museum, set back from Mission Street and fronted by a lovely plaza, looks like a traditional brick building—until you see the two steel shapes wedged into its side.

Clockwise from far left: The striking Koret-Taube Grand Lobby; eye-catching lighting in the Stephen and Maribelle Leavitt "Yud" Gallery; one of the vast steel shapes wedged into the brick building; a view of the museum from Mission Street

The museum's approach isn't quite traditional, either. It doesn't have a permanent collection—instead it stages temporary exhibitions relating to Jewish art, film, music and more. The museum explores a range of themes about the Jewish identity and spirit. It also features performances and education programs, including a number of activities and events for kids.

Encouraging participation Exhibits here include interactive elements whenever possible. For example, a recent exhibit was set up as a nightclub, featuring café tables with a "menu" of songs, along with iPad listening stations. In another exhibit, a professionally trained female scribe (they're usually male) spent more than a year at the museum writing out the text of the Torah in an open studio.

THE BASICS

www.thecjm.org

🚩 Q5

✉ 736 Mission Street between 3rd and 4th

☎ 415/655–7800

🕐 Mon-Tue, Fri-Sun 11–5, Thu 11–8

🚇 Montgomery

🚌 14, 30, 45

♿ Good

💰 Moderate; free to under-18s; inexpensive Thu after 5pm

HIGHLIGHTS

● *Ocean Park: Variation #8*, Diebenkorn
● *Storm in the Rocky Mountains*, Bierstadt
● *The Ironworkers' Noontime*, Anshutz
● *Mrs. Daniel Sargent*, Copley
● *Three Machines*, Thiebaud
● *A Dinner Table at Night*, Singer Sargent
● Philadelphia High Chest of Drawers
● Observation floor of the 144ft (44m) tower

From Amish quilts to the couture of Spain's Balenciaga, this museum stocks diverse exhibits from around the world. Exemplary collections of American painting and decorative art are the main draw.

Paintings After several years of waiting in great anticipation, the de Young Museum returned home to Golden Gate Park in 2005, reopening in a stunning new building. The museum's collection of American paintings begins with the 18th-century society portraits of John Singleton Copley and his contemporaries. From here, the museum traces the growing self-confidence of American artists and the lessening importance of European trends. By the mid-1800s, many American artists were taking inspiration from the newly settled West: The landscapes of

Clockwise from far left: The de Young Museum returned to Golden Gate Park in 2005; the larger-than-life Man Observing Series II *(1984), by Viola Frey; taking a rest in the American Gallery; the museum at night*

Albert Bierstadt and the sculpture of Frederick Remington evoke the period's celebratory mood of expansion. By contrast, Richard Diebenkorn's work is a strikingly Californian contribution to 1960s and '70s contemporary art.

Furnishings The furniture, too, reflects the US's historic shift from colony to nation as it moves from English and Dutch armchairs used in New England settlements of 1670 to a Federal-period parlor from 1805 Massachusetts. The flowing curves of the Queen Anne style were popular during the colonial period but by the time of the revolution, American craftsmen had acquired the skills and creativity to evolve a new look. Philadelphia emerged as the center of the craft, and a grand 1780 Philadelphia High Chest provides an excellent example of the period.

THE BASICS

http://deyoung.famsf.org

✚ F7

✉ 50 Hagiwara Tea Garden Drive, Golden Gate Park

☎ 415/750–3600

🕐 Tue–Sun 9.30–5.15 (some Fri until 8.45)

🍴 Café

🚌 5, 21, 44, N–Judah

♿ Excellent

💷 Moderate; includes the Legion of Honor (▷ 48–49) if visited on same day. Free 1st Tue of month. Observation tower free

❓ Free tours daily. Lectures, films

HIGHLIGHTS

- Tactile Dome
- Wave Organ
- Alien Voices
- Anti-gravity Mirror
- Bright Black
- Tune Blocks
- Distorted Room
- Shadow Box
- Soap Film Painting
- Momentum Machine

DID YOU KNOW?

- Construction has begun on brighter, more spacious quarters at Piers 15 and 17, on the Embarcadero. The museum is due to move to this new location in 2013.

Without a doubt the best place in San Francisco to amuse young minds with low boredom thresholds, the Exploratorium sets the pace for hands-on museums across the US.

Questions and answers Founded by Frank Oppenheimer, who worked alongside his more famous brother, Robert, on the development of the atomic bomb in the 1940s, the Exploratorium occupies a single vast hall and has 650 hands-on, interactive exhibits designed to illustrate and explain the fundamentals of natural science and human perception in a user-friendly environment. Helpful "explainers" stroll around answering questions, and new exhibits are developed in a workshop open to public view. The odd bits of statuary you might

There are plenty of hands-on activities to amuse youngsters at the Exploratorium, including the Particle Accelerator (below) and the Liquid Mirror (bottom)

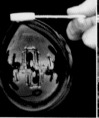

spot gathering dust in the corners are remnants of the building's original role as part of the Palace of Fine Arts (▷ 54–55).

Innovative art and science Be they crackling tesla coils or coupled resonant pendulums, the permanent exhibits stand alongside a series of temporary installations. These have included "Listen: Making Sense of Sound", which enables visitors to explore how they perceive sound, and "Traits of Life," an interactive presentation on the essentials of biology. An innovative artist-in-residence program has resulted in many imaginative artworks based on scientific themes. The Exploratorium's most popular exhibit is the Tactile Dome, a dark "tunnel" from which participants can leave only by feeling their way out on their hands and knees.

THE BASICS

www.exploratorium.edu

✚ J2

✉ 3601 Lyon Street

☎ 415/563-7337; recorded information 415/EXPLORE (or 415/397-5673); Tactile Dome reservations 415/561-0362

🕐 Tue–Sun 10–5; also Mon public hols

🍴 Cafeteria

🚌 28, 29, 30, 43

♿ Excellent

💲 Expensive; free 1st Wed of month. A ticket including entry to the Tactile Dome is more expensive

- Miette pastries
- Blue Bottle Coffee
- Cowgirl Creamery's Artisan Cheese Shop
- The Ferry Building's steel-trussed glass ceiling
- The Farmers' Market

TIP

- There's validated parking across the street at the Washington Embarcadero lot. On weekdays, valet parking is available in front of the Ferry Building.

After an extensive renovation in the 1990s, the Ferry Building and central waterfront have become center stage once again. In addition to being a transit hub, the Ferry Building also houses a large marketplace, with shops and cafés selling pastries, fresh meat, artisan cheeses, flowers and more.

Survivor's story The Ferry Building opened in 1898 and its 245ft-high (75m) clock tower was for many years the city's tallest structure. Surviving the 1906 earthquake and fire—and a plan to demolish it for safety reasons during the disaster—the slender clock tower became a symbol of San Francisco's ability to survive natural catastrophe. Ironically, another natural disaster—the 1989 Loma Prieta earthquake—actually helped the Ferry Building. The unsightly

Clockwise from far left: Looking up at Four Embarcadero; the Ferry Building's clock tower survived the 1906 earthquake; outdoor sculpture at the Embarcadero Center; the Farmers' Market; a view across the water toward the Embarcadero and Financial District; inside the Ferry Building

Embarcadero Freeway was damaged and later removed, restoring the views and the natural beauty of the waterfront.

Community hub The marketplace has a range of shops, cafés and restaurants (everything from upscale Vietnamese to burgers), while the building is also a transit hub for ferries, MUNI and BART. On Tuesday, Thursday and Saturday, the Ferry Plaza Farmers' Market sells fresh produce, flowers and more, drawing big crowds.

Stroll the Embarcadero Head south along the palm-lined Embarcadero to take in the views of the Bay Bridge and the water, and to see *Cupid's Span*, a sculpture by Claes Oldenburg and Coosje van Bruggen. It's a reference to Tony Bennett's *I Left My Heart in San Francisco*.

THE BASICS

www.ferrybuildingmarket
place.com

➕ R4

✉ Foot of Market Street, at the Embarcadero

☎ 415/983–8030

🕐 Mon–Fri 10–6, Sat 9–6, Sun 11–5. Ferry Plaza Farmers' Market Tue, Thu 10–2, Sat 8–2

Ⓜ Embarcadero

🚌 2, 6, 9, 14, 21, 31, F

♿ Good

🎫 Free

DID YOU KNOW?

● Weight of bridge, anchorages and approaches: 887,000 tons
● Actual bridge length: 6,450ft (1,966m)
● Length of central span: 4,200ft (1,280m)
● Height above water: 220ft (67m) at low tide
● Height of towers above water: 746ft (227m)
● Color: International Orange, the color most easily distinguishable in fog
● Gallons of paint used annually: 5,000 (22,727L)
● Annual vehicle crossings: more than 42 million

Named for the entrance to San Francisco Bay rather than its color, the Golden Gate Bridge must be the most recognizable, and the most beautiful, of all the bridges in the United States.

Artful engineering The bridge is a remarkable feat of artistry as well as engineering. The construction overcame the exceptional depth and strong currents of the Golden Gate, while the simple but inspired design allows it to elegantly connect the city to the hillsides of Marin County.

Loathed but then loved A bond issue of $35 million was authorized in 1930 to finance the bridge's construction, amid great antipathy from San Franciscans, many of whom feared

The Golden Gate Bridge is an iconic sight as it spans San Francisco Bay, dwarfing the yachts that sail under it

that it would result in a loss of the beauty of the Golden Gate. An early design by the project's chief engineer, Joseph B. Strauss, was likened to "two grotesque steel beetles emerging from either bank." The design that was eventually adopted is thought to have been the work of Strauss's assistants. The affection the bridge now enjoys was confirmed in 1987 when 200,000 people filed onto it to mark the 50th anniversary of its opening.

Fatal attraction On a more downbeat note, the Golden Gate Bridge has become a notorious spot for suicides. The first occurred three months after the bridge's opening. In 2010 alone there were 32 confirmed incidents of people jumping the 220ft (67m) from the central span to the raging waters below.

THE BASICS

www.goldengatebridge.org

✚ E–F1

🕐 Open to pedestrians daily 5am–9pm (5am–6pm in winter). Open to vehicles 24 hours a day

🚌 28, 76

♿ Good at observation platform

✋ Free for pedestrians and bicyclists. Inexpensive toll for city-bound drivers

13 Golden Gate National Recreation Area

HIGHLIGHTS

- Coastal trail
- China Beach
- Baker Beach
- Fort Point (▷ 69)
- Seal Rocks
- Fort Funston
- Marin Headlands
- Crissy Field
- Ocean Beach
- Golden Gate Promenade

TIP

- Baker Beach is the perfect spot for a rest.

An enormous swath of mostly undeveloped land lying within the city and extending northward across the Golden Gate Bridge, the Golden Gate National Recreation Area is a good reminder of how open most of California is.

Creation From the cliffs of Fort Funston in the south to the hills of Marin County in the north, the Golden Gate National Recreation Area bestows federal protection on a long chunk of San Francisco's coastline. The area's 75,500 acres (30,553ha), which lie in separate pockets and often lack clearly marked boundaries, were created in 1972 by the amalgamation of city parks, private land and former military-owned areas. Abandoned fortifications include a Civil War fort (Fort Point, ▷ 69, located beneath the

Clockwise from far left: White foaming surf hits Seal Rocks; walkers, runners and bicyclists enjoy views of the Golden Gate Bridge at Crissy Field; you may be lucky enough to spot sea lions at Seal Rocks

Golden Gate Bridge) and a massive World War II cannon at Baker Beach.

Exploration Much of Golden Gate NRA is best explored on foot. Start at the Cliff House, close to the sea lion-frequented Seal Rocks. Walk the coastal trail that weaves through the coarsely vegetated hillsides, which rise steeply above the tiny beach of Lands End and the forbidding waters of the Golden Gate. All vestiges of the city are hidden until the appearance of the Golden Gate Bridge. This route also brings views of China Beach, named for the Chinese fishermen of the Gold Rush era who lived in shacks beside it. China Beach is one of the few San Francisco beaches safe for swimming. Crissy Field, formerly a military airfield, was restored to tidal marsh and beaches in 2001.

THE BASICS

www.nps.gov/goga

✛ E3, G2

🛈 415/561–4700

🕐 Daylight hours only recommended

🍴 Beach Hut Café, 1199 East Beach; daily 9–5 (also has tourist leaflets)

🚌 5, 18, 19, 28, 29, 30, 31, 38, 48, 76 travel to various parts of the GGNRA

♿ Range from none to excellent according to location

💲 Free

HIGHLIGHTS

- Conservatory of Flowers
- Japanese Tea Garden
- Windmills
- Stow Lake
- California Academy of Sciences

TIP

● If you're traveling with children, try a boat ride on Stow Lake (☎ 415/752–0347) or a ride on the carousel, which was at the 1939 World's Fair on Treasure Island.

Once a desolate stretch of sand dunes, Golden Gate Park is now a massive slab of greenery holding several museums. It's also a stage from which San Francisco, and its jogging, kite-flying, roller-skating population, presents its playful side to the world.

Acres of fun Some 3.5 miles (5.6km) long and half a mile (1km) wide, Golden Gate Park is one of the world's largest urban parks. Within its 1,000 acres (405ha) is the de Young Museum (▷ 30–31), the California Academy of Sciences (▷ 18–19) and many other major attractions, plus a polo field, golf course, archery range, botanical garden, lakes, waterfalls, two windmills and a bison paddock. Yet there is still sufficient space to become hopelessly lost amid tree-shrouded lanes and footpaths.

Clockwise from far left: Pagodas in the Japanese Tea Garden; strolling in the Strybing Arboretum; vividly colored callistemon (bottlebrush) flowers; rowing on Stow Lake; the Dutch Windmill in the Queen Wilhelmina Tulip Garden

On foot The park is too large to cover entirely on foot but the eastern half is fine for strolling. Here you'll find the redstone McLaren Lodge, former office of the park's creator and now an information center (maps are essential), and the AIDS Memorial Grove, a 7.5 acre (3ha) wooded grove and scene of private services following the loss of a loved one to AIDS. Nearby is the Conservatory of Flowers (▷ 68), with its tropical vegetation, and the Japanese Tea Garden (▷ 70–71), with azaleas, cherry trees and a carp-filled pond. West of the Tea Garden a road encircles Stow Lake, at the center of which Strawberry Hill rises to a 400ft (122m) summit. South of the Tea Garden is the San Francisco Botanical Garden at Strybing Arboretum (▷ 74), which offers free guided walks daily at 1.30 (also 10.30 on weekends).

THE BASICS

www.golden-gate-park.com

➕ F7

✉ Bordered by Great Highway, Lincoln Way, Fulton and Stanyan streets

☎ 415/831–2700

🕐 Daylight hours only recommended

🍴 Tea at Japanese Tea Garden; cafés at de Young Museum and California Academy of Sciences

🚌 5, 18, 21, 28, 29, 33, 44, 71, N–Judah

♿ Good

💲 Park free

ℹ Park Visitor Center: Beach Chalet, 1000 Great Highway (at western end of park, just south of Fulton Street), tel 415/386–8439; Mon–Fri 9–4

DID YOU KNOW?

● Huntington Park, facing the cathedral, is named for railroad baron Collis P. Huntington.

It would be nice to think that Grace Cathedral, located as it is on the site of a former robber-baron's Nob Hill mansion, provides some spiritual atonement for the materialist excesses that characterize the neighborhood.

Slow building When the mansion of railroad boss Charles Crocker was destroyed by the fire that followed San Francisco's 1906 earthquake, the Crocker family donated the land to the Episcopalian church. Although the cathedral's cornerstone was laid in 1910, construction did not begin until 1928, and further delays (due partly to the Depression) resulted in Grace Cathedral's consecration being postponed until 1964. Described by its main architect, Lewis P. Hobart, as "a truly American cathedral," the

Highlights of Grace Cathedral include the stained-glass windows (left and far left) and the gilded bronze doors (bottom), from the same cast as the Gates of Paradise doors in Florence's Baptistery

cathedral is in fact neo-Gothic in style, partly modeled on Notre-Dame in Paris.

Through the doors The most impressive part of the exterior is a pair of gilded bronze doors from the Lorenzo Ghiberti cast that was used for the Gates of Paradise doors of the Baptistery in Florence. Inside, a 15th-century French altarpiece and an exquisite Flemish reredos can be seen in the Chapel of Grace, while the stained-glass windows depict biblical scenes and diverse achievers such as Albert Einstein and Henry Ford. The cathedral has, controversially, frequently hosted radical figures invited to speak from its pulpit. There are two labyrinths at the cathedral, one outdoors and one indoors. Both are modeled after the famous labyrinth at Chartres Cathedral in France.

THE BASICS

www.gracecathedral.org

✚ P4

✉ 1100 California Street at Taylor Street

☎ 415/749–6300

🕐 Sun–Fri 7–6, Sat 8–6

🚋 1; California Street cable car

♿ Good

❓ Free tours daily, usually before and after services. Occasional lectures; exhibitions on social issues and concerts—check the website for details

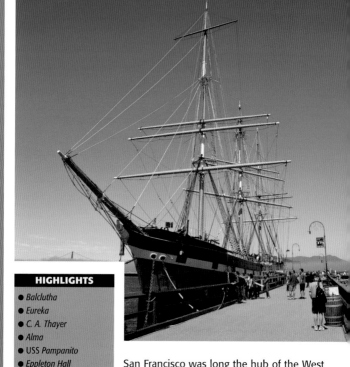

HIGHLIGHTS

- *Balclutha*
- *Eureka*
- *C. A. Thayer*
- *Alma*
- USS *Pampanito*
- *Eppleton Hall*
- Maritime bookstore

TIP

● Currently only the lobby and scenic veranda of the nearby art deco Maritime Museum (Beach Street, at the foot of Polk Street) are open, displaying a few models and paintings of ships. Renovations of the upper floors will take several years, but additional exhibits may be on display in 2012.

San Francisco was long the hub of the West Coast's maritime trade, and the vessels docked at Hyde Street Pier, as part of the San Francisco Maritime National Historical Park, provide a reminder of the city's seafaring heyday.

Cape Horn veteran The grandest of the ships is the *Balclutha*, a steel-hulled, square-rigged ship launched in Scotland in 1886. This vessel, originally intended to carry wheat between California and Europe, rounded Cape Horn 17 times before ending its days transporting Alaskan salmon along the West Coast. Clamber down the ladders and around the decks for a look at the restored cabins, including the elegant saloon enjoyed by the ship's master, and to read the informative explanatory texts.

Clockwise from far left: The 1895 Schooner C. A. Thayer; the square-rigged Balclutha *transported wheat between Europe and California; people walk past a large model of an old sea dog; the* Balclutha, *docked at Hyde Street Pier*

Boats of the bay The 1940s cars and trucks on the lower decks of the *Eureka* suggest the era when the vessel was the world's largest passenger ferry and able to haul 2,300 people and 120 vehicles between San Francisco and Sausalito in a single trip. The other exhibits are the *C. A. Thayer*, built in 1895 to move the lumber used in the construction of many early Californian cities; a 1907 deep-water steam tug, *Hercules*; a paddle tug dating from 1914, *Eppleton Hall*, which spent its working life towing barges in Britain; and the *Alma*, a scow schooner built in 1891, whose flat bottom enabled her to navigate the shallow waters of the bay. The restored USS *Pampanito*, a World War II submarine that made six patrols in the Pacific, is part of the National Park but located at Pier 45.

THE BASICS

www.nps.gov/safr/index.htm

www.maritime.org/pamphome.htm

🚹 N1

✉ Aquatic Park, Hyde Street

☎ 415/447–5000

🕐 Daily 10–5

🚌 19, 30; Hyde–Powell cable car

♿ Few

💲 Inexpensive

17 Japantown

HIGHLIGHTS

● National Japanese American Historical Society
● Japan Center
● Cherry Blossom Festival

TIP

● For two weekends in April, Japantown comes alive with the annual Cherry Blossom Festival, featuring a street fair of Japanese arts and crafts, martial artists, *taiko* drummers and cooking demonstrations.

Today, comparatively few Japanese live in Japantown, bordered by Octavia and Fillmore streets, and O'Farrell and Pine streets, but it's still the spiritual home of San Francisco's Japanese-Americans.

History Established in the late 1800s, San Francisco's Japanese-American community was the first in the US, spanning 30 blocks of the Western Addition. In 1941 almost all the city's 7,000 Japanese-Americans lived and worked here. America's entry into World War II, following the Japanese attack on Pearl Harbor, led to the government's forced internment of the US's Japanese citizens; when the war ended many didn't return to Japantown. California passed legislation in 2001 to preserve the three remaining Japantowns in the state.

Clockwise from far left: The Peace Pagoda stands out against a brilliant-blue sky; the unusual Origami Fountain; taking a break at the Japan Center; if you fancy some Japanese cuisine, there are plenty of restaurants to choose from; a clothes store in the Japan Center

Exhibits and shops At the National Japanese American Historical Society (▷ 72) you can explore the Japanese-American experience. The area's commercial hub is the large Japan Center (Post and Buchanan streets), two indoor malls connected by Peace Plaza. The Miyako and Kintetsu malls house Japanese restaurants and shops selling everything from samurai figurines to Japanese books and foods.

Japanese architecture Across Post Street is the pedestrian-only block of Buchanan Street designed by Japanese-American Ruth Asawa. Several churches have Japanese-style architecture, including Soto Zen Mission Sokoji (Laguna Street), Konko Church of San Francisco (Bush Street), founded in 1931, and the Buddhist Church of San Francisco (1881 Pine Street).

THE BASICS

www.sfjapantown.org
www.njahs.org
➕ L5
🍴 Plenty of choice, including Mifune (▷ 147)
🚌 2, 3, 22, 38

HIGHLIGHTS

● *Old Man*, de La Tour
● *The Tribute Money*, Rubens
● *St. John the Baptist*, El Greco
● *The Thinker*, Rodin
● *The Three Shades*, Rodin
● *Trotting Horse*, Degas
● *The Grand Canal, Venice*, Monet
● View of Golden Gate

Rodin and San Francisco may seem an unlikely combination, but fans of the French sculptor enjoy a visit to this hill-top building that has many of his works amid a fine collection of European art.

Sugar money The collection in the Legion of Honor (modeled on the Légion d'Honneur Museum in Paris) was started in the 1910s by Alma Spreckels, wife of millionaire San Franciscan sugar magnate, Adolph. Already passionate about European art, Alma met Rodin in Paris and began a lasting interest in his work. Her husband, meanwhile, was motivated to open an art museum through his bitter rivalry with another prominent San Franciscan family, the de Youngs, who had founded the de Young Museum (▷ 30–31).

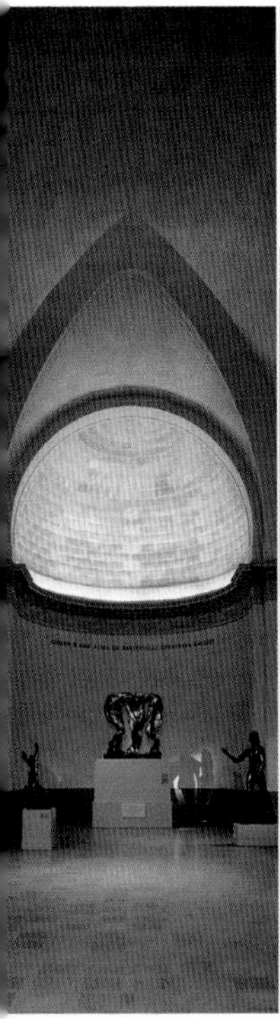

Clockwise from far left: Rodin's The Thinker *ponders life in the Court of Honor; sculpture on display in Gallery 10; paintings in Gallery 18; artworks in the Early Northern European Gallery; a view of the museum from across the pond*

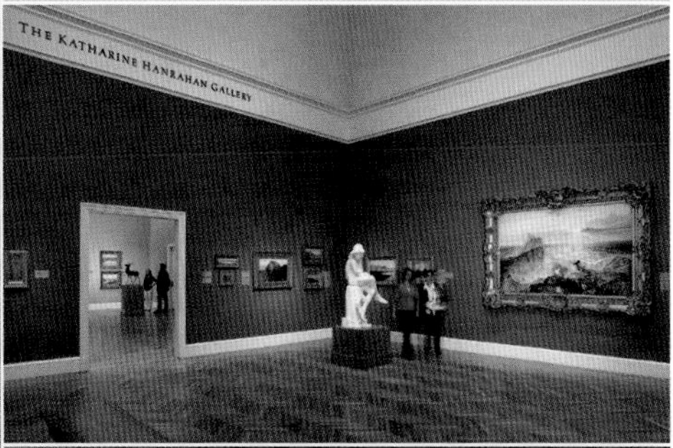
THE KATHARINE HANRAHAN GALLERY

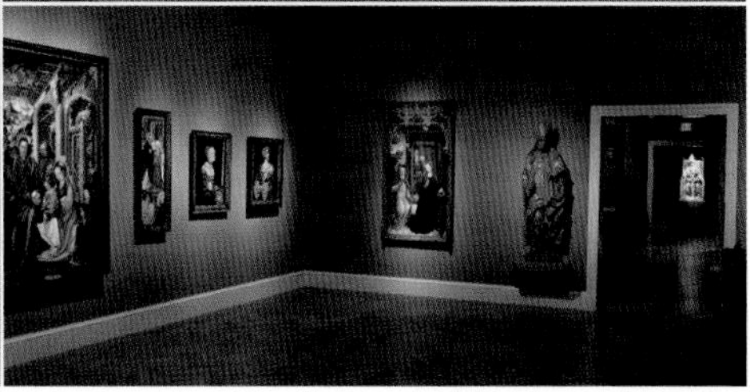

The collections *The Three Shades* and *The Thinker* stand in the grounds, and some 70 other Rodin works are inside the museum. The general galleries, meanwhile, are arranged in a chronological sequence from the medieval period to the early 20th century, with the highlights mostly from the 18th and 19th centuries. Downstairs, the Achenbach Foundation for Graphic Arts holds more than 100,000 prints and some 3,000 drawings by artists as diverse as Albrecht Dürer and Georgia O'Keeffe, and selections are shown in short-term exhibitions (otherwise by appointment). The Legion also gets first-rate traveling exhibitions; recent ones have included the Magna Carta, on loan from Oxford's Bodleian Library. Outside, beside the parking lot, be sure to see George Segal's *Holocaust* sculpture.

THE BASICS

http://legionofhonor.famsf.org

B5

Lincoln Park

415/750-3600

Tue–Sun 9.30–5.15

Café

1, 2, 18, 38

Good

Moderate; free 1st Tue of month

Check the website for special event information

19 Mission Dolores

DID YOU KNOW?

- Full name: Misión San Francisco de Asís
- Founded: 1776
- Building commenced: 1782
- Building completed: 1791
- Length: 114ft (35m)
- Width: 22ft (7m)
- Thickness of walls: 4ft (1.5m)
- Number of adobe bricks: 36,000
- First earthquake-proofing measures: 1918

Evidence of the 18th-century Spanish settlement of California rarely surfaces in today's San Francisco, but Mission Dolores, the oldest building in the city, provides visitors with a welcome insight into the era.

California's missions The mission was the sixth in a chain of 21 built by the Spanish across California. From San Diego to Sonoma, each mission was located a day's horse ride from the next. The Spaniards' intention was to convert Native Americans to Catholicism, to utilize their labor and to earn their support in colonial conflict. Mexico's independence from Spain in 1821 put the sparsely populated California in Mexican hands, and resulted in the decline and secularization of many of the missions. Most were restored by the US government.

Clockwise from far left: A statue of Junipero Serra stands amid the trees and flowers; the newer basilica, with its ornate Churrigueresque facade, was completed in 1918; sculptures adorn the basilica's exterior; inside the 18th-century chapel

Inside the mission Passing through the thick adobe walls, largely responsible for the mission's success in withstanding numerous earthquakes, you enter the small and richly atmospheric chapel, which has an altar dating from 1780 and is decorated with frescoes by Native Americans. A modest assortment of historic pieces is gathered in the mission's museum, the oldest being a baptismal register for 1776. In the cemetery, headstones mark Spanish- and Mexican-era notables, while the Lourdes Grotto indicates the common grave of some 5,000 Native Americans—many of whom were killed by diseases brought by the colonists. Next to the chapel is the far larger basilica, completed in 1918, now used for Sunday Mass and most weddings; the chapel is used for daily Mass and baptisms.

THE BASICS

www.missiondolores.org

➕ M8

✉ 320 Dolores Street (entrance 3321 16th Street)

☎ 415/621–8203

🕐 Daily 9–4 (May–Oct until 4.30)

🚇 16th Street–Mission

🚌 33, 49

♿ Few

💲 Donation

HIGHLIGHTS

● *Yosemite Valley*, Bierstadt
● Diebenkorn paintings
● *Migrant Mother*, Lange
● *San Francisco, July 1849*, Burgess
● Interactive animation and sound-effects studios
● 1913 Cadillac
● 1925 gas pump
● Sculpture garden

TIP

● For advice on sensible precautions to take when in Oakland, ▷ 169–170.

If you cross the San Francisco Bay, don't ignore Oakland. It's home to this superb museum, which leads the way in documenting the history, nature and art of the Golden State.

History Every episode in California's past is remembered here. The collections are enhanced by computers providing recorded commentaries from experts. From outlining the conflicts between Californians and the colonizing Spaniards, the collections come up to date with the rise of Californian computer companies, the invention of the mountain bike and the role of Hollywood.

Californian art An imaginative selection of exhibits demonstrates how the art of California

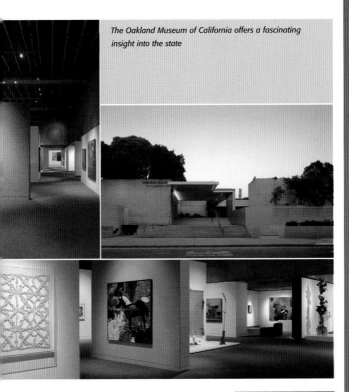

The Oakland Museum of California offers a fascinating insight into the state

has developed from 19th-century depictions of its untamed, natural beauty, through to the self-confidence of 20th-century artists such as semi-abstract painter Richard Diebenkorn and ceramicist Peter Voulkos. The photography collection has outstanding contributions from Dorothea Lange and Maynard Dixon, both of whom were based in San Francisco.

Nature The museum's Natural Sciences Gallery will return in the spring of 2012, when the museum completes its renovation. It will explore the remarkable plant and animal life found in the high mountains, low deserts, beneath the ocean and in the other habitats of California. In the meantime, explore the peaceful outdoor sculpture garden, with its views of Lake Merritt.

THE BASICS

www.museumca.org

➕ Off map to east

✉ 1000 Oak Street, Oakland

☎ 510/238–2200, 888/625–6873

🕐 Wed–Thu, Sat–Sun 11–5, Fri 11–9

🍴 Café

🚇 Lake Merritt

♿ Excellent

💲 Moderate; free 1st Sun of month

❓ Free tours. Films, lectures and events

DID YOU KNOW?

- Architect: Bernard Maybeck
- Built: 1915
- Inspirations: Böcklin's *Isle of the Dead*; the drawings of Piranesi
- Materials: originally plaster and wood on a chicken-wire frame
- Height of rotunda: 160ft (49m)
- First restoration: 1964–1975
- Second restoration completed: 2010
- Original cost: $621,929

The Palace of Fine Arts is one of the most beautiful structures in San Francisco. Remarkably, it was intentionally built as a ruin and serves no practical purpose whatsoever.

Architects' playtime In 1915, ostensibly to mark the opening of the Panama Canal, San Francisco announced its recovery from the devastation of the 1906 earthquake and fire by staging the Panama Pacific International Exposition. A group of noted architects was commissioned to erect temporary structures to house the Expo on land reclaimed from the bay. One of the architects was Bernard Maybeck, and it was his Palace of Fine Arts more than any other building that captured the imagination of the Expo's 19 million visitors.

The Palace of Fine Arts was not intended to be a permanent feature of the city when it was built in 1915, but it captured the imagination of San Franciscans and visitors alike

Although it was intended as a temporary structure and was built mostly of plaster and chicken wire, the Palace of Fine Arts aroused such public affection that it was preserved and then, in the 1960s, replicated in concrete at a cost of $7.5 million. In 2010, a $21-million restoration, which included a new dome roof, landscaping and seismic upgrades, was completed.

Art in ruins Maybeck designed a Roman ruin, using a classical domed rotunda as the structure's centerpiece and flanking this with a fragmented colonnade. Each group of columns was topped by weeping maidens and decorated by aimless stairways and huge urns. The intention was to prepare visitors for the classical art exhibited in the Expo's Great Hall (now housing the Exploratorium, ▷ 32–33).

THE BASICS

www.lovethepalace.org

🞣 J2

✉ 3601 Lyon Street

🕐 Always open

🚌 28, 30

♿ None

✋ Free

HIGHLIGHTS

● *Woman with the Hat*, Matisse
● *Woman*, Willem de Kooning
● *Land's End*, Jasper Johns
● *Guardians of the Secret*, Pollock
● *Violin and Candlestick*, Braque
● Paul Klee drawings
● *The Flower Carrier*, Rivera
● Clyfford Still gallery
● East European photography
● The rooftop garden

Striking and sympathetic architecture, outstanding collections and innovative temporary exhibitions make SFMOMA a showplace befitting a forward-thinking city.

Main attraction The core of the museum's permanent collection highlights painting and sculpture from 1900 to 1970. Among significant contributions from Europeans are Pablo Picasso's *Head in Three-quarter View* and *The Coffee Pot,* and Georges Braque's *Violin and Candlestick.* Do not miss Matisse's *Woman with the Hat,* painted in 1905; a work that made a crucial contribution to what became the century's first radical art movement—fauvism. Abstract expressionist canvases include Jackson Pollock's *Guardians of the Secret,* contributions from Willem de Kooning, and the last work by

Clockwise from far left: The museum looms up behind a sculpture of an upturned ship, by John Roloff, in Yerba Buena Gardens; giant columns in the atrium; the rooftop garden pavilion; looking up through a futuristic bridge to the sky above

Barnett Newman. Latin-American artists also feature; among the best are intriguing Mexican modernists Diego Rivera and Frida Kahlo.

Other galleries With exhibits spread across six floors, the museum has much space to devote to California art. The canvases of Richard Diebenkorn have particular relevance to the region, as do the 28 works donated by California-based abstract expressionist Clyfford Still. The Phyllis Wattis Theater (main floor) has film screenings, artist lectures and other presentations. The museum is also equipped to stage provocative exhibitions in the emerging fields of video, computer and interactive art. A $480-million expansion is underway, part of which will house the collection of Donald and Doris Fisher, cofounders of clothing retailer Gap.

THE BASICS

www.sfmoma.org

🔲 Q5

✉ 151 3rd Street

☎ 415/357–4000

🕐 Sun–Tue, Fri–Sat 10–5.45, Thu 10–8.45; shorter hours in winter

🍴 2 cafés

Ⓜ Montgomery

🚌 12, 30, 45, 76

♿ Excellent

💲 Expensive; free 1st Tue of month

DID YOU KNOW?

- Architect: William L. Pereira & Associates
- Smallest floor: 48th, 45ft (14m) per side
- Largest floor: 5th, 145ft (44m) per side
- Angle of slope: 5 degrees
- Number of floors: 48

TIP

- Transamerica Redwood Park, behind the Transamerica Pyramid, stages free lunchtime concerts on weekdays.

A recognized landmark worldwide, the Transamerica Pyramid is San Francisco's most distinctive building and arguably the most innovative modern contribution to the city's skyline.

Perfect profile With a construction cost of $32 million, San Franciscans were slow to appreciate the splendor of the 853ft-high (260m) building's unique profile. Rising above the Financial District's forest of even-sided high-rises, with a slowly tapering spire flanked by windowless wings and with a decorative spire rising for 212ft (65m) above the 48th floor, the Transamerica Pyramid adds greatly to the city skyline and has steadily been accepted since 1972. The current owner is the Dutch insurance company Aegon, who acquired

The Transamerica Pyramid dominates the San Francisco skyline, by day and by night

the Transamerica corporation, which grew from various companies built around the Bank of Italy (later renamed the Bank of America), which was established in San Francisco in 1904.

Inside Construction took place between 1969 and 1972. To help withstand earthquakes, the structure sits on a steel and concrete block sunk 50ft (15m) into the ground. It has 18 elevators, two of which reach the top, and 3,678 windows. The building is a place of business for the more than 1,500 employees of the 50 firms who rent its space. Since September 11, 2001, unfortunately, the lobby and building have been closed to the general public, so the bird's-eye views of the city are no longer accessible, and visitors must admire the structure from afar.

THE BASICS

www.thepyramidcenter.com

🏠 Q4

✉ 600 Montgomery Street

🕐 Open to employees and their approved guests only

🚌 30, 41

❓ Lobby and building closed to visitors post-9/11

HIGHLIGHTS

- Sproul Plaza
- Campanile (also called Sather Tower—carillon recitals on Sunday afternoons)
- Hearst Mining Building
- Phoebe A. Hearst Museum of Anthropology
- Berkeley Art Museum and the Pacific Film Archive
- Sather Gate
- Lawrence Hall of Science
- Morrison Library
- Bancroft Library

A haven of 1960s student dissent, the University of California Berkeley campus might be less radical than it once was, but its buildings and museums and the picture it provides of contemporary student life easily justify a trip.

Past The first college at Berkeley opened in the 1850s, but a lack of funds allowed the facility to be purchased in 1873 by the state government as the first of what are now 10 campuses of the University of California. Much of the university's early finance came as donations from Phoebe Apperson Hearst, wife of a wealthy mining baron and mother of the even more wealthy publishing tycoon William Randolph Hearst. In the 1940s, Robert Oppenheimer was UC Berkeley's professor of physics before moving

Clockwise from far left: The Haas School of Business, at the east side of the campus; the Commencement Convocation at the Greek Theatre marks the pinnacle of the students' achievements; Sather Gate and the Campanile; the Heyns Reading Room, in the Doe Library

to Los Alamos to work on the first atomic bomb. In 1964 the seeds of what evolved into countrywide student rebellions were sown by the sit-ins and rallies of Berkeley's Free Speech Movement.

Present UC Berkeley's 35,000 or so students are now more interested in acquiring a good degree than radical politics, though there is no shortage of campaigns being promoted along Sproul Plaza, in the heart of the campus. Elsewhere on the 178-acre (72ha) campus are museums, libraries and architecturally distinguished buildings, such as John Galen Howard's beaux-arts-style Hearst Mining Building. Howard was also responsible for the elegant Sather Gate, marking the main entrance to the campus opposite Telegraph Avenue.

THE BASICS

www.berkeley.edu

✚ Off map to northeast

✉ Main Gate, Bancroft Way

☎ 510/642–5215

🕐 Daylight hours recommended. Tours Mon–Sat 10, Sun 1

Ⓟ Berkeley

♿ Good

💲 Free

❓ In 2013 the Berkeley Art Museum, currently at 2626 Bancroft Way, is due to move to Oxford Street, along the western edge of the campus

HIGHLIGHTS

- San Francisco Museum of Modern Art (▷ 56–57)
- Esplanade and Martin Luther King Memorial
- Center for the Arts
- Museum of the African Diaspora (▷ 72)
- Children's Creativity Museum (▷ 67)
- Carousel
- Cartoon Art Museum (▷ 66–67)
- St. Patrick's Church
- Metreon (▷ 136)
- Contemporary Jewish Museum (▷ 28–29)

An infusion of culture in the shadow of Financial District towers, Yerba Buena Gardens are the green heart of a still-evolving tract that mixes museums and arts venues with commercial spaces.

The past In the 1970s, declining manufacturing industries were encouraged to vacate the factories south of Market Street. The opening of the Moscone Convention Center in 1981 became the first step in the regeneration of an under-exploited area within walking distance of the city center.

The present Snaking through the landscaped greenery of Yerba Buena Gardens, the Esplanade is decorated with wacky sculptures and passes an artificial waterfall enclosing a

Yerba Buena Gardens offer the chance to take time out from the bustle of city life. Highlights include the Martin Luther King, Jr. Memorial (below, behind the waterfall), and a range of museums and other cultural venues

monument to Martin Luther King. Adjacent, the Center for the Arts was completed in the mid-1990s with a 775-seat theater, an outdoor auditorium and several galleries with exhibitions of contemporary art. Across Third Street rises the landmark Museum of Modern Art (▷ 56–57). The grey block of the Metreon (▷ 136) forms the Garden's west side, close to which a 1916 carousel marks the approach to the Children's Creativity Museum (▷ 67). St. Patrick's Church, built in 1892 for the once-immense Irish population, is across Mission Street.

Latest additions Joining diverse institutions such as the California Historical Society and the Cartoon Art Museum (▷ 66–67) are the city's Contemporary Jewish Museum (▷ 28–29) and the Museum of the African Diaspora (▷ 72).

THE BASICS

www.ybca.org
www.yerbabuenagardens.com

➕ Q5

✉ Bounded by 3rd, 4th, Mission and Howard streets

☎ 415/978–2787

⏱ Ask about individual attractions

🚇 Montgomery Street or Powell Street

🚌 10, 12, 30, 38, 45

♿ Excellent

💰 Esplanade free; varies for individual attractions

More to See

This section contains other great places to visit if you have more time. Some are in the heart of the city while others are a short journey away, found under Further Afield. This chapter also has fantastic excursions that you should set aside a whole day to visit.

MORE TO SEE

In the Heart of the City

MORE TO SEE

555 CALIFORNIA STREET

www.555california.com

Formerly known as the Bank of America Center, this is a supreme example of inspired 1960s high-rise office architecture. The 52-story building's dark red exterior, dominating the area by day, seems to become almost transparent at sunset.

➕ Q4 ✉ 555 California Street 🚌 1, 30; California Street cable car

ALAMO SQUARE

Perhaps the most photographed view in San Francisco is of the six Victorian homes, or "painted ladies," on the east side of Alamo Square contrasting with the modern towers in the background.

➕ L6 ✉ Bordered by Hayes, Fulton, Scott and Steiner streets 🚌 5, 21, 22, 24

ASIAN ART MUSEUM

www.asianart.org

Housing the largest collection of its kind in the US, this museum was located in Golden Gate Park for many years. It reopened in the city's former main library in 2003,

the larger space enabling many more of its 17,000 objects to be displayed. The exhibits span 6,000 years and diverse cultures and religions, but the major collections are from China and include the oldest dated example of Chinese Buddhist art (AD338), and important items from the Ming Dynasty (1368–1644) and Xuande Era (1426–35). But the smaller and less obvious items can also delight, such as the silver work, wood carvings and textiles from Bhutan, which bring a rare insight into this obscure country.

➕ N6 ✉ 200 Larkin Street, Civic Center ☎ 415/581-3500 🕐 Tue–Sun 10–5 (also Thu until 9 Feb–Sep) 🚇 Civic Center 🚌 5, 19, 21, 47, 49 ♿ Excellent 💲 Moderate; free 1st Sun of month

CARTOON ART MUSEUM

www.cartoonart.org

Be they from comics, TV or the movies—or culled from the deepest recesses of history—cartoons are accorded the seriousness of art in the changing exhibitions staged here, which seldom fail to be

The exhibits at the Asian Art Museum span 6,000 years

thought-provoking and entertaining. Displays cover artists from Hanna-Barbera to Charles Schulz. The museum has a classroom for cartoon art and a bookstore with books, gifts and prints.

🚼 Q5 ✉ 655 Mission Street ☎ 415/227–8666 🕐 Tue–Sun 11–5 🚇 Montgomery 🚌 Any Market Street bus, also 10, 30, 45 ✋ Moderate

CHESTNUT STREET

www.chestnutshop.com
A mix of shops, eateries and bars have given this Marina District street an effervescent mood and a reputation as a haunt of the young, affluent and unattached.

🚼 K–L2 ✉ Between Divisadero and Fillmore streets (for shops and restaurants) 🚌 30

CHILDREN'S CREATIVITY MUSEUM

www.childrenscreativitymuseum.org
This arts and technology museum, formerly known as Zeum, encourages kids to use interactive exhibits. There are two floors and six studio spaces where visitors

are encouraged to explore their creative side, whether that involves making a music video, sculpting characters in clay or learning about digital art. In front of the museum, a restored 1906 carousel by Charles Looff—featuring a menagerie of beautifully hand-carved animals—offers rides for all ages.

🚼 Q6 ✉ 221 4th Street ☎ 415/820–3320 🕐 Wed–Fri 1–5, Sat–Sun 11–5; longer hours weekdays in summer; carousel daily 11–6 🚌 14, 30, 45 ✋ Moderate

CHINATOWN

www.sanfrancisco.chinatown.com
The compact streets and alleyways of Chinatown's 24 history-laden blocks are home to one of the largest Asian communities outside Asia. Several 100-year-old temples, fortune-cookie factories and numerous exotic stores are crammed into one of the city's most energetic and ethnically distinct neighborhoods. The area also holds some of the city's best-value restaurants.

🚼 P4 🚌 1, 30, 45; also California Street cable car

Outdoor dining on busy Chestnut Street

Colorful umbrellas and lanterns decorate a shop in Chinatown

CHINESE CULTURE CENTER

www.c-c-c.org

On the third floor of the towering Hilton San Francisco—which looms above Portsmouth Square and its legions of elderly Chinese men indulging in games of chance—are rotating exhibitions that explore diverse aspects of Chinese culture.

➕ Q4 ✉ Hilton San Francisco, 750 Kearny Street ☎ 415/986-1822 🕐 Tue–Sat 10–4 🚌 15, 30, 45

CHURCH OF SAINTS PETER AND PAUL

www.stspeterpaul.san-francisco.ca.us

Long the place of worship for North Beach's Italian community, this imposing Romanesque edifice was founded in 1922. The twin spires rise above Washington Square and are evocatively illuminated at night.

➕ P3 ✉ 666 Filbert Street ☎ 415/421-0809 🕐 Usually 7.30am–8pm 🚌 30, 39, 41, 45 💧 Free

CONSERVATORY OF FLOWERS

www.conservatoryofflowers.org

The Conservatory of Flowers is arranged by themed galleries:

aquatic plants, highland tropics, lowland tropics, potted plants and the special exhibits gallery. More than 50 countries and 1,700 plant species from tropical forests are represented.

➕ G7 ✉ JFK Drive, Golden Gate Park ☎ 415/666-7001 🕐 Tue–Sun 10–4 🚌 5, 21, 33, 44, 71, N–Judah 💧 Moderate; free 1st Tue of month

DIEGO RIVERA GALLERY

http://diegoriveragallery.com

An immense mural by the Mexican master Diego Rivera sits at one end of this gallery of the highly respected San Francisco Art Institute, while student works line the other three walls.

➕ N2 ✉ 800 Chestnut Street ☎ 415/771-7020 (Ext. 4410) 🕐 Daily 9–5 🚌 30, 41; Powell–Hyde cable car

FORT MASON CENTER

www.fortmason.org

From the time of San Francisco's 18th-century Spanish *presidio* (or garrison) to the Korean War of the 1950s, Fort Mason served a military role. From 1972, however,

The Conservatory of Flowers has plants from more than 50 countries

the troop barracks were steadily transformed into a vibrant cultural center. Visual arts can be seen at the Museo ItaloAmericano, focusing on Italian-American topics, and the San Francisco Museum of Modern Art Artists Gallery. Photography, painting and sculpture are also likely to be on show at other spaces around the center. Fort Mason is also home to several theaters, including BATS Improv (▷ 133), the Magic Theatre (▷ 136) and the Young Performers Theatre.

➕ M2 ✉ Marina Boulevard at Laguna Street (cars enter at Marina Boulevard at Buchanan Street) ☎ 415/345–7500 🕐 Individual museums and galleries vary 🍴 Greens vegetarian restaurant (▷ 144) 🚍 22, 28, 30, 49 ♿ Few 💲 Individual museums free or inexpensive

FORT POINT NATIONAL HISTORIC SITE

www.nps.gov/fopo/index.htm
Completed in 1861, Fort Point was intended to deter enemy incursions into San Francisco Bay during the Civil War and World War II but never a shot was fired in anger. Period-attired guides describe the fort's past.

➕ F1 ✉ Beneath south end of Golden Gate Bridge ☎ 415/556–1693 🕐 Fri–Sun 10–5 🚍 28, 29, 76

GHIRARDELLI SQUARE

www.ghirardellisq.com
One of Fisherman's Wharf's successful conversions, the red-brick shell of the chocolate factory that opened here in 1893 now holds a strollable complex of shops and restaurants.

➕ N2 ✉ 900 North Point Street 🚍 19, 30; Powell–Hyde cable car

GLIDE MEMORIAL CHURCH

www.glide.org
The Sunday celebration at Glide is the main draw (Bill Clinton famously came to a service), as is the Reverend Cecil Williams. Being inclusive is the goal, and the services focus on community, music and spirituality—you'll be encouraged to sing along with the Glide Ensemble and the eight-piece Change Band, to dance,

Fort Point National Historic Site

Ghirardelli Square

and to hold hands with the person next to you, whether they're a stranger or a loved one. People of all religious backgrounds feel the uplifting spirit of the celebrations. Note that Glide fills up fast on Sundays; arrive 30 minutes early to make sure you get a seat.

➕ P5 ✉ 300 Ellis Street ☎ 415/674–6000 🕔 Sun 9am, 11am 🚇 Powell 🚌 27 💲 Free

HAAS-LILIENTHAL HOUSE

www.sfheritage.org/haas-lilienthal-house
This elaborate 1886 example of Queen Anne-style architecture is also the only San Franciscan Victorian building to retain its period-furnished rooms. Knowledgeable tour guides help bring to life the history and architectural details of the house and share anecdotes about previous owners. Today Haas-Lilienthal is owned by the non-profit San Francisco Architectural Heritage.

➕ M4 ✉ 2007 Franklin Street ☎ 415/441-3000 🕔 Guided tours Wed, Sat 12–3, Sun 11–4 🚌 3, 19, 47 💲 Moderate

HAIGHT-ASHBURY

Holding hundreds of elegant Victorian homes that survived the 1906 earthquake, and becoming world famous as the heart of hippiedom in 1967, Haight-Ashbury has long been the most tolerant section of a tolerant city. It has vintage clothing outlets and bookstores, and is a center for alternative lifestyles.

➕ J8 🚌 6, 33, 43, 66, 71

HAYES VALLEY

This once-seedy neighborhood morphed into an attractive shopping and dining destination after the 1989 Loma Prieta earthquake damaged the unsightly freeway that blighted the neighborhood. High-end restaurants and burger joints coexist now, along with chic boutiques and galleries.

➕ M6 ✉ Hayes Street between Franklin and Laguna streets 🚌 21

JAPANESE TEA GARDEN

http://japaneseteagardensf.com
Laid out in traditional Japanese style, the garden was the work of

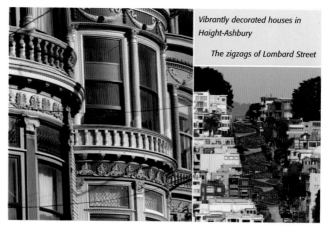

Vibrantly decorated houses in Haight-Ashbury

The zigzags of Lombard Street

Makoto Hagiwara, who was interned after the 1941 Japanese attack on Pearl Harbor.

➕ F7 ✉ Hagiwara Tea Garden Drive and Martin Luther King Jr. Drive ☎ 415/666-3232 🕐 Mar–Oct daily 9–6; Nov–Feb 9–4.45 🚌 5, 21, 33, 44, 71, N–Judah 💺 Inexpensive

LOMBARD STREET

Traffic zigzags slowly down Lombard Street, "the crookedest street in San Francisco," moving around colorful gardens put in place in the 1920s. On busy summer days, cars back up on Lombard all the way to Van Ness Avenue as drivers wait to head down the crooked street. Go early or late, if possible.

➕ N2 ✉ Between Hyde and Leavenworth streets 🚌 19, 30

MAIDEN LANE

Notorious for its brothels in the 1800s, this road is now lined with smart stores and bordered by fancy white gates. During the late 1940s, architect Frank Lloyd Wright undertook a complete remodeling of 140 Maiden Lane and the design provided a foretaste of his acclaimed Guggenheim Museum in New York. The exterior brickwork is imbued with Mayan motifs; go inside to find the distinctive spiral ramp.

➕ Q5 ✉ Between Stockton and Kearny streets 🚌 2, 3, 30, 45

MARINA GREEN

Kite-flying, jogging and the walking of dogs are among the popular pursuits in this bay-side green strip, overlooked by pastel-colored stucco-fronted houses and serving an affluent neighborhood. This 74-acre (30ha) stretch of grass also offers fantastic views of the Golden Gate Bridge, Alcatraz and Angel Island.

➕ K–L2 ✉ Beside Marina Boulevard 🚌 22, 76

MISSION DISTRICT MURALS

www.precitaeyes.org, www.balmyalley.com Some of the best of the Mission District's many murals, reflecting Latin-American muralist traditions, line Balmy Alley and focus on a

Murals on the Women's Building, in the Mission District

theme of peace in Central America. Visit during daylight.

⊞ Off map at P9 ⊠ Balmy Alley, between 24th and 25th streets ☎ Precita Eyes Mural Center: 415/285–2287 (telephone for tour schedule) 🚌 12, 27, 67

MUSEUM OF THE AFRICAN DIASPORA (MOAD)

www.moadsf.org

Celebrating and exploring the contributions made by those of African descent, MoAD tells its stories through photographs, art, "first voice" narratives, lectures, interactive exhibits and more. Permanent exhibits touch on topics such as slavery, culinary traditions, adornment and music.

⊞ Q5 ⊠ 685 Mission Street ☎ 415/358–7200 🕐 Wed–Sat 11–6, Sun 12–5 🚌 14, 30, 45 💲 Moderate

NATIONAL JAPANESE AMERICAN HISTORICAL SOCIETY

www.njahs.org

In the heart of Japantown, the changing exhibitions here document varied aspects of the Japanese-American life over several generations, including the community's contribution to sport, the military, dining and the legacy of unfair internment during World War II.

⊞ L5 ⊠ 1684 Post Street ☎ 415/921–5007 🕐 Mon–Fri 12–5 and 1st Sat of month 🚌 2, 3, 76

NOB HILL

A quartet of extremely wealthy Californians (the "Big Four") built the first million-dollar mansions on Nob Hill from the 1870s. The 1906 earthquake and fire destroyed all but one of the district's opulent homes, but Nob Hill's pedigree is still evident. The area is home to exclusive hotels and a very well-dressed congregation shows up for Sunday services at the neighborhood's Grace Cathedral (▷ 42–43).

⊞ P4 🚋 1, 27; California Street cable car

NORTH BEACH

North Beach's wealth of cafés and bookstores recall its links with the Beat Generation of the 1950s.

Houses on Nob Hill

North Beach has plenty of Italian restaurants

Meanwhile, the abundant Italian-owned restaurants and stores are reminders of the Italians who settled in the district in force from the late 19th century.

➕ P2 🚌 30, 39, 41, 45

OCTAGON HOUSE

This is one of five eight-sided houses in San Francisco, their shape considered lucky by the owners. The Octagon House dates from 1861 and the restoration program was organized by the Colonial Dames of America, whose exhibitions of Colonial- and Federal-period arts and crafts now fill the interior.

➕ M3 ✉ 2645 Gough Street ☎ 415/441–7512 🕐 Tour 2nd Sun and 2nd and 4th Thu of month 12–3 🚌 41, 45 🎫 Free

OLD ST. MARY'S CATHEDRAL

www.oldsaintmarys.org

The West Coast's first Catholic cathedral and the forerunner of today's ultramodern St. Mary's Cathedral (▷ this page), Old St. Mary's was completed in 1854.

➕ Q4 ✉ 660 California Street ☎ 415/288–3800 🕐 Mon–Fri, Sun 7.30–6, Sat 12–6 🚌 1, 30; California Street cable car 🎫 Free

ST. MARY'S CATHEDRAL

www.stmarycathedralsf.org

The cathedral's towering, gleaming-white hyperbolic paraboloids give it a ceiling 194ft (59m) high and form the shape of a Greek cross. Inside, the open-plan cathedral can seat 2,400 people. Its design is intended to eliminate the usual divisions between a cathedral's different areas. Here, the apse, nave, transepts, baptistery and narthex are undivided beneath the tall ceiling, in the center of which is a skylight in the shape of the Cross. The four stained-glass windows that rise from floor to ceiling in each main wall represent the four elements.

Note: To avoid interrupting Mass, call ahead for the schedule.

➕ M5 ✉ 1111 Gough Street ☎ 415/567–2020 🕐 Mon–Sat 6.45–5, Sun 7.30–5 🚌 2, 3, 38 ♿ Excellent 🎫 Free

Old St. Mary's Cathedral...

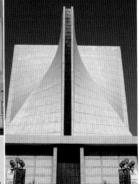

...and the strikingly modern St. Mary's Cathedral

SAN FRANCISCO BOTANICAL GARDEN AT STRYBING ARBORETUM

www.sfbotanicalgarden.org

More than 7,500 varieties of outdoor plants from around the globe fill 55 tended acres (22ha). See the state's famous redwoods on the Redwood Trail.

F8 ✉ Ninth Avenue at Lincoln Way ☎ 415/661–1316 🕐 Apr–Oct daily 9–6; Nov–Mar 10–5 🚌 44, 71, N–Judah 🖐 Moderate

SUTRO HEIGHTS PARK

From the former grounds of the home of legendary 19th-century San Francisco benefactor Adolph Sutro are fabulous views of the Pacific coast and the western end of Golden Gate Park. Remnants of the house and its statuary are scattered about the park.

A6 ✉ Bordered by Point Lobos Avenue, Great Highway and 48th Street 🚌 18, 38

TEMPLE EMANU-EL

www.emanuelsf.org

This immense Byzantine-style structure looms above the surrounding residential architecture. Finished in 1926 at a cost of $3 million, the temple serves the longest-established Jewish congregation in the Bay Area.

H5 ✉ Lake Street and Arguello Boulevard ☎ 415/751–2535 🕐 Call for guided tour information 🚌 1, 33 🖐 Free

UNION STREET

The affluent, fashionable residents of Pacific Heights shop, eat and socialize along these chic blocks. The charming Victorian setting makes shopping here a delight.

L3 ✉ Between Franklin and Steiner streets 🚌 22, 41, 45

THE WALT DISNEY FAMILY MUSEUM

www.waltdisney.org

Parents might hear "Disney" and assume this museum is for kids, but while there are animated clips and interactive elements that kids will like, the exhibits on the life of Walt Disney will be more interesting to adults. The 10 galleries focus on his life, from his art classes in Kansas City, Missouri, to the creation of Mickey Mouse. Highlights include an elaborate model of Disneyland and lots of audio and video clips. A downstairs screening room shows Disney classics twice daily (extra charge).

H2 ✉ 104 Montgomery Street, the Presidio ☎ 415/345–6800 🕐 Wed–Mon 10–6 🚌 43 🖐 Excellent 🖐 Expensive

WELLS FARGO MUSEUM

www.wellsfargohistory.com/museums

A leading US financial institution, the name of Wells Fargo is synonymous with the early days of the American West, and this collection demonstrates the historic links. A few steps from the site of the company's 1852 office, the Wells Fargo Museum (inside the Wells Fargo Bank) entertainingly documents the rise of the company. Sitting inside an 1860s stagecoach provides one highlight, but there is much more to see amid the clutter of a re-created Gold Rush-era Wells Fargo office: gold-weighing scales, bulky mining tools, gold coins and aging letters that miraculously survived their trip across the rutted tracks of the old West.

Q4 ✉ 420 Montgomery Street ☎ 415/396–2619 🕐 Mon–Fri 9–5 🚌 1, 41; California Street cable car 🖐 Good 🖐 Free

Further Afield

ANGEL ISLAND STATE PARK
http://angelisland.org
For a day in the wilds, make the short ferry crossing from Fisherman's Wharf to the mile-square (2.5sq km) Angel Island. The largest piece of land in San Francisco Bay, the island is a state park with paths and bicycle trails. You can also visit a former immigration processing center and see the remains of a military prison. Ferry companies sailing to the island include Tiburon Ferry, Blue & Gold Fleet, and Hornblower Cruises.
➕ Off map to north ✉ 1 mile (1.5km) south of Tiburon Peninsula ☎ 415/435–5390 🕐 Daily 8am–dusk 💲 Expensive (fee for ferries)

CASTRO
www.castrosf.org
The Castro neighborhood, near Noe Valley and the Mission, flies its gay flag proudly—and literally. Castro Street, the main drag, has restaurants, gay bars (including Twin Peaks Tavern, one of the oldest gay bars in the city, at 401 Castro) and the illustrious Castro

Theatre (▷ 133). In the 1970s the street was home to Harvey Milk's camera shop, which doubled as his campaign headquarters.
➕ L9 ✉ Castro Street 🚌 24, 33, 35, 37, F, L, K

NOE VALLEY
Strollers (pushchairs) and dogs abound in this neighborhood near the Mission District. The commercial stretch is 24th Street, with tempting restaurants and shops selling everything from high-end cheeses to Latin-American imports.
➕ Off map to south ✉ 24th Street between Guerrero and Diamond streets 🚌 24, 35, 48, J-Church

SAN FRANCISCO ZOO
www.sfzoo.org
Awkwardly located on the fringes of the city, this zoo holds the usual complement of creatures, plus Penguin Island.
➕ Off map to southwest ✉ Sloat Boulevard and 45th Avenue ☎ 415/753–7080 🕐 Mid-Mar to early Nov daily 10–5; early Nov to mid-Mar 10–4 🚌 18, 23, L 💲 Expensive

The former Immigration Station at Angel Island State Park

Penguins are among the animals you can see at San Francisco Zoo

Excursions

SAN JOSE

www.sanjose.org

California's third-largest city, San Jose is also known as the "capital" of Silicon Valley. After a dramatic population and housing boom in the latter half of the 20th century, San Jose's primary industry shifted from agriculture to high-tech. Today San Jose has a larger population than San Francisco and has some sights worth visiting.

San Jose's Tech Museum of Innovation features interactive exhibits organized by themes including innovation, renewable energy, the human body and exploration. The museum also houses an IMAX Dome Theater. The Rosicrucian Egyptian Museum and Planetarium displays an intriguing assemblage of amulets, mummies, textiles, scrolls and other antiquities from the cultures of Assyria, Babylon and Egypt.

Travelers with kids could stop by the Winchester Mystery House. Widow and rifle heiress Sarah Winchester believed that the spirits of those killed by Winchester weapons haunted her; if her house was ever completed, she was certain she would die. So her carpenters spent 38 years building this 160-room Victorian mansion. There are stairways to nowhere and windows that open to blank walls, plus 47 fireplaces.

Nearby is Santana Row (between Olsen Drive and Stevens Creek Boulevard), a shopping and entertainment destination with nearly two dozen restaurants, 70 stores and a luxurious day spa.

Winchester Mystery House

Distance: 50 miles (80km) south of San Francisco
Journey Time: 1 hour
Route: Take US 280 south to the Vine Street/Almaden Boulevard exit. Turn left onto Almaden Boulevard
🛈 408 Almaden Boulevard ☎ 408/295–9600 or 800/726–5673

Tech Museum of Innovation
www.thetech.org
✉ 201 South Market Street ☎ 408/294–8324 🕐 Mon–Wed 10–5, Thu–Sun 10–8
💰 Moderate

Rosicrucian Egyptian Museum and Planetarium
www.egyptianmuseum.org
✉ 1660 Park Avenue ☎ 408/947–3636
🕐 Wed–Thu 9–5, Fri 9–8, Sat–Sun 10–6
💰 Moderate

Winchester Mystery House
✉ 525 South Winchester Boulevard
☎ 408/247–2101 🕐 Daily at 8am (summer), 9am (winter); closing time varies
💰 Expensive

SAUSALITO

www.sausalito.org

Once inundated with fishermen, bordellos and gambling dens, Sausalito has morphed into a summer escape for the elite of San Francisco, which these days thrives on tourism.

Bridgeway is the main thoroughfare, running along the promenade past the ferry landing and shops, which include a number of galleries. The street also has waterfront restaurants. The Bay Model Visitor Center, on Marinship Way, is a replica of the San Francisco Bay and a scientific tool operated by the US Army Corps of Engineers. The Bay Area Discovery Museum on McReynolds Road has interactive exhibits and multimedia labs to entice children to learn about art, science and media. Its Lookout Cove also has 2.5 acres (1ha) of space for outdoor playing.

Over at Cavallo Point resort, adults can improve their culinary skills at the Cavallo Point Cooking School or enjoy the lauded Murray Circle restaurant. Visitors can also hike around Fort Baker, under the Golden Gate Bridge.

Frigid temperatures in the San Francisco Bay make swimming an activity to avoid, but Sea Trek Sausalito rents single and double kayaks and offers guided trips.

Distance: 12 miles (19km) north of San Francisco
Journey Time: 30 minutes
Route: Take US 101 north, exit at Alexander Avenue on the north end of the Golden Gate Bridge. Follow signs to downtown Sausalito 🚹 780 Bridgeway ☎ 415/332–0505 🚢 Blue & Gold Fleet from Pier 39 at Fisherman's Wharf or the Golden Gate Ferry departing from the San Francisco Ferry Building 🚌 Golden Gate Transit Bus 10

Bay Model Visitor Center

www.spn.usace.army.mil

✉ Marinship Way, parallel to Bridgeway ☎ 415/332–3871 🕐 Jun–Aug Tue–Fri 9–4, Sat–Sun 10–5; Sep–May Tue–Sat 9–4 ✋ Free

Bay Area Discovery Museum

www.baykidsmuseum.org

✉ 557 McReynolds Road ☎ 415/339–3900 🕐 Tue–Fri 9–4, Sat–Sun 10–5 ✋ Moderate

Cavallo Point

www.cavallopoint.com

✉ 601 Murray Circle ☎ 415/339–4700

Sea Trek Sausalito

www.seatrek.com

✉ Schoonmaker Point Marina (at the end of the marina) ☎ 415/332–8494

An aerial view of Sausalito harbor

SONOMA VALLEY

www.sonomavalley.com

Entire guidebooks are devoted to the Wine Country, but visitors can get a good feel for the region by exploring the lovely Sonoma Valley, which is less commercial than nearby Napa Valley. When visiting vineyards in the area, note that in addition to wine tasting, wineries often have other activities and events, including cave tours, tram rides and food-and-wine pairing dinners. During Wine Country's "crush" harvest season, usually mid-August to October, the area is particularly beautiful, busy and packed with special events. It's wise to plan ahead.

While in the town of Sonoma, explore the Sonoma Mission and the other restored historic buildings, artisan shops and boutiques around Sonoma Plaza. A few minutes from the plaza is Buena Vista Winery and Tasting Room. North of Sonoma is the hamlet of Glen Ellen, where visitors can tour Jack London State Historic Park, the former home of the writer whose name it bears. Continue north to Kenwood, where there are more wineries, including Chateau St. Jean and Kunde Family Estate. About 25 miles (40km) north of Kenwood is the small town of Healdsburg, which has a charming town square, a variety of restaurants and a number of wineries within a 20-minute radius.

For a non-winery detour northwest of Kenwood, head to the town of Santa Rosa, just off Highway 101. There you'll find the Charles M. Schulz Museum and Research Center, which features the art of the cartoonist behind the "Peanuts" strip, and a re-creation of his studio.

Sonoma City Hall

Distance: 45 miles (72km) north of San Francisco

Journey Time: 1 hour

Route: Take the Golden Gate Bridge and continue north on US 101 through San Rafael and follow signs to the town of Sonoma

🛈 453 1st Street East ☎ 866/996–1090 or 707/996–1090

Jack London State Historic Park

✉ 2400 London Ranch Road ☎ 707/938–5216 🕐 Thu–Mon 10–5 💲 Moderate (vehicle fee)

Charles M. Schulz Museum

www.schulzmuseum.org

✉ 2301 Hardies Lane, Santa Rosa 🕐 Jun–Aug Mon–Fri 11–5, Sat–Sun 10–5; Sep–May Mon, Wed–Fri 11–5, Sat–Sun 10–5

STANFORD UNIVERSITY

www.stanford.edu

Venture south from San Francisco to reach Stanford University, an 8,180-acre (3,310ha) campus in the Silicon Valley featuring sandstone and tile architecture.

While students and locals refer to the school as "the Farm," the prestigious private university has blue blood. Founded by Leland Stanford, a railroad magnate and US senator, in memory of his only son, the university boasts the third-largest endowment in the nation. Famous former students include Chelsea Clinton, Tiger Woods and the founders of HP and Google.

Campus walking tours (lasting 70 minutes) are offered at 11am and 3.15pm daily, except during the university's winter break and other holidays. Tour highlights include the Main Quad, dominated by Hoover Tower. Rising 285ft (87m) and completed in 1941, the tower is named for the country's 31st president, who was a member of the first graduating class of 1895. It was built to mark the university's 50th anniversary.

Art-lovers should stop by the Cantor Arts Center and the adjoining Rodin Sculpture Garden. The galleries showcase art spanning the centuries, from the *Torso of Dionysos* (AD50) to Rodin sculptures to modern and contemporary works; an additional 20 bronze Rodin sculptures are on display in the Rodin Sculpture Garden (open 24 hours).

Get lunch on campus at Cool Café, overlooking the Rodin Sculpture Garden.

Distance: 33 miles (53km) south of San Francisco
Journey Time: 40 minutes
Route: Take US 101 south to Embarcadero Road exit heading west toward Stanford. At El Camino Real, turn into Galvez Street as it enters the university. Stay in the left lane and continue to the heart of campus
🛈 Memorial Hall, Serra Street (across from Hoover Tower) ☎ 650/723–2560
Cantor Arts Center
✉ Lomita Drive and Museum Way
☎ 650/723–4177 🕐 Wed, Fri–Sun 11–5, Thu 11–8 🍴 Cool Café 💲 Free

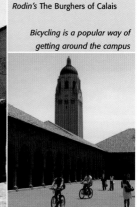

Rodin's The Burghers of Calais

Bicycling is a popular way of getting around the campus

City Tours

This section contains self-guided tours that will help you explore the sights in each of the city's regions. Each tour is designed to take one or two days, with a map pinpointing the recommended places along the way. There is a quick reference guide at the end of each tour, listing everything you need in that region, so you know exactly what's close by.

CITY TOURS

The Presidio

Old meets new in the Presidio, where several remarkable symbols—the Legion of Honor, the Palace of Fine Arts and the famed Golden Gate Bridge—share space with George Lucas's Letterman Digital Arts Center and The Walt Disney Family Museum, the district's most recent addition.

Morning
Begin your tour of the Presidio area with its most iconic landmark, the **Golden Gate Bridge** (▷ 36–37). Head to the base of the span by foot, bike or car, then stroll across the pedestrian lane and take in the city views. Back at the base of the southern edge of the bridge, stop into **Fort Point National Historic Site** (▷ 69) to learn a bit about San Francisco's military history—and to see lovely beach views and an unexpected angle of the bridge: its underbelly.

Mid-Morning
Recharge at the **Warming Hut** (Presidio Building 983; daily 9–5; longer in summer), a café and bookstore at the western end of Crissy Field, near the Golden Gate Bridge, where you can get a caffeine fix, a snack and souvenirs. Then head to the **Palace of Fine Arts** (▷ 54–55) to see the dome, the duck-filled lagoon and, on weekends, most likely a bridal party taking wedding pictures. Next is the **Exploratorium** (▷ 32–33), an engaging, hands-on museum that answers science questions for kids, but also entertains adults (note that in 2013, the museum is moving to Piers 15 and 17, on the Embarcadero).

Lunch
Geary Boulevard is the main artery of the Richmond District, home to ethnic restaurants serving authentic cuisine at reasonable prices. Try **Ton Kiang** (▷ 149) for high-quality dim sum, or stumble on another gem in the area. Clement Street, which runs parallel to Geary, also has good restaurant choices. **Burma Superstar** (309 Clement Street; daily lunch and dinner) always has a wait, for good reason.

Afternoon

Investigate more of the **Golden Gate National Recreation Area** (▷ 38–39), a protected area that attracts 17 million visitors annually.

Mid-Afternoon

Wind your way through the Presidio to **The Walt Disney Family Museum** (▷ 74), which chronicles the history and triumphs of one of America's most famous animators. Audio and video footage of Disney, his family, his colleagues and his beloved creations bring him to life. Highlights include drawings, movie clips, a tribute to Snow White and an elaborate model of Disneyland.

Dinner

The best option for dinner is sophisticated **Spruce** (▷ 148–149), in Laurel Heights. While the area isn't known for its nightlife, diners can stay at Spruce for a cocktail in the lively bar area, or check out the **Presidio Social Club** (▷ 148). Families looking for an evening activity could reserve one of the 12 lanes at **Presidio Bowl** (Presidio Building 93, Moraga Avenue and Montgomery Street; Sun–Thu 9am–midnight, Fri–Sat 9am–2am), which also serves food and drinks.

Golden Gate Bridge

Fort Point National Historic Site

Fort Point Wharf

Warming Hut

Marine Drive

East Drive

Battery

LINCOLN

Hoffman Street

Armistead Road

Langdon Court

Merchant Road

BOULEVARD

DOYLE

Storey Avenue

LINCOLN

Fort Winfield Scott

Cowley

Kobbe Avenue

Ralston Avenue

Dynamite Road

Ruckman Avenue

Pilcher Avenue

Upton Street

Appleton Street

Ord Street

Kobbe Avenue

Boulevard

Golden Gate National Recreation Area

World War II Memorial

Washington Boulevard

Hitchcock

Wright Loop

Infantry

Central Magazine Road

Compton Road

Boulevard

Washington

Armatury

Park Boulevard

Presidio

BOULEVARD

LINCOLN

Stilwell Road

Pershing Drive

Wedemeyer Street

Baker Beach

Bowley Street

Baker Court

Brooks Street

Hays Street

Barnard Avenue

Sheridan

Girard Road

Palm Avenue

Lincoln Boulevard

Legion of Honor

Sea Cliff Avenue

El Camino Del Mar

28th Avenue

Scenic Way

Mountain Lake

Mountain Lake Park

SEA CLIFF

West Clay Street

LAKE

Lake Street

Camino Del Mar

California

Sutro Annex Park

PARK

PRESIDIO

BOULEVARD

CALIFORNIA

Clément Street

Clement Street

Tacoma Street

GEAR

Sutre Heights Park

GEARY BOULEVARD

Ton Kiang

GEARY BOULEVARD

CENTRAL RICHMOND

Anza

Anza Street

Balboa Street

Balbo

26th Avenue · 27th · 26th · 25th · 24th · 23rd · 22nd · 21st · 20th · 19th · 18th · 17th · 16th · 15th · 14th · Funston · 12th · 11th · 10th · 9th

AVENUE

| 0 | 500 m |
| 0 | 500 yds |

D   E   F

84

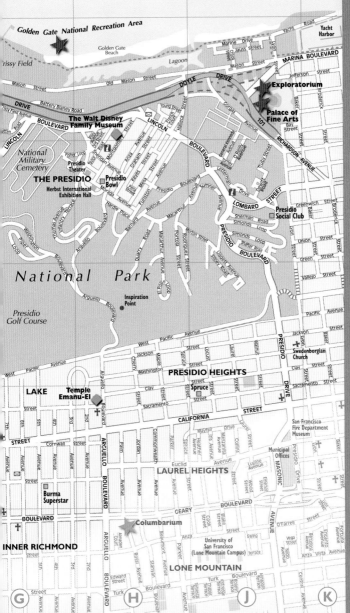

San Francisco Bay

Golden Gate National Recreation Area

Golden Gate Beach

Trissy Field

Lagoon

MARINA BOULEVARD

Yacht Harbor

Marine Drive

Jauss Street

Mason Street

Old Mason Street

DOYLE DRIVE

Jefferson Street

Lyon Street

Baker

Broderick

101

Exploratorium

Palace of Fine Arts

RICHARDSON AVENUE

Bay Street

LINCOLN BOULEVARD

Battery Blaney Road

Trissy Field Avenue

DRIVE

Young Street

LINCOLN

The Walt Disney Family Museum

BOULEVARD

National Military Cemetery

THE PRESIDIO

Fisher Loop

Presidio Theater

Presidio Bowl

Herbst International Exhibition Hall

Montgomery Street

Anza Avenue

Graham Street

Keyes Avenue

Mesa Street

Funston Avenue

Presidio Boulevard

Hardie Place

Barnard Avenue

Macarthur Avenue

Letterman Drive

Lombard Street

Gorgas Avenue

LOMBARD

Presidio Social Club

Greenwich Street

Sherman Road

Simonds Loop

Lincoln Boulevard

Lombard

Torney Avenue

Infantry Terrace

Presidio Boulevard

Quarry Road

ELPaso Road

Portola Street

Rodriguez Street

Morton Street

Amatury Loop

PRESIDIO

Simonds Loop

Shafter Road

BOULEVARD

Baker Street

Broderick

Lyon Street

Union Street

Green Street

Vallejo Street

National Park

Arguello Boulevard

Park Boulevard

Washington Boulevard

Inspiration Point

Pacific Avenue

Jackson Street

Presidio Golf Course

West Pacific Avenue

West Pacific Avenue

LAKE

Temple Emanu-El

Street

7th Avenue

6th Avenue

5th Avenue

4th Avenue

3rd Avenue

Cornwall Street

Arguello Boulevard

2nd Avenue

West Pacific Avenue

Jackson Street

Washington Street

Maple Street

Cherry Street

Arguello Boulevard

Spruce Street

Locust Street

Laurel Street

Walnut Street

PRESIDIO DRIVE

Jackson Street

Swedenborgian Church

Clay Street

Sacramento Street

Baker Street

Lyon Street

PRESIDIO HEIGHTS

Spruce Street

Clay Street

Sacramento Street

CALIFORNIA STREET

San Francisco Fire Department Museum

Palm Avenue

Jordan Avenue

Commonwealth Avenue

Parker Avenue

Spruce Street

Mayfair Drive

Iris Avenue

Heather Avenue

Collins Street

Maple Street

Laurel Street

Walnut Street

Locust Street

LAUREL HEIGHTS

Euclid Avenue

Lupine Avenue

Masonic Avenue

Wood Street

Emerson Street

Municipal Offices

PRESIDIO DRIVE

Baker Street

Burma Superstar

BOULEVARD

GEARY BOULEVARD

Cook Street

Blake Street

Anza Street

O'Farrell Street

Vega Street

Wood Street

Fortuna Avenue

Encanto Avenue

Barcelona Avenue

Anza Vista Avenue

INNER RICHMOND

5th Avenue

4th Avenue

3rd Avenue

2nd Avenue

ARGUELLO BOULEVARD

Edward Street

Stanyan Street

Rossi Avenue

Beaumont Avenue

Parker Avenue

Almaden Court

Columbarium

University of San Francisco (Lone Mountain Campus)

Terrace

Ewing Terrace

Chabot Terrace

Central Avenue

Vega Street

LONE MOUNTAIN

Turk Boulevard

Turk Street

Boulevard

Edward Street

5th Avenue

4th Avenue

Street

G   H   J   K

The Presidio Quick Reference Guide

 SIGHTS AND EXPERIENCES

Exploratorium (▷ 32)
Children learn about the fundamentals of natural science and human perceptions in a hands-on, friendly environment. Hundreds of interactive exhibits put the fun into science.

Golden Gate Bridge (▷ 36)
Both a feat of engineering and beauty, the span connecting San Francisco to Marin County is the most recognizable bridge in the country. More than 42 million vehicles cross it every year.

Golden Gate National Recreation Area (▷ 38)
From stunning cliffs to rugged coastline, the GGNRA comprises 75,500 acres (30,553ha) of protected land on both sides of the Golden Gate Bridge.

Legion of Honor (▷ 48)
This stately hill-top museum houses a fine collection of European art, including more than 70 works by Rodin, along with a diverse collection of prints and drawings.

Palace of Fine Arts (▷ 54)
A Roman-style ruin that was built for the Panama Pacific International Exposition in 1915, the Palace of Fine Arts was meant to be temporary, but an adoring city has helped it survive.

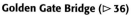

The Byzantine-style Temple Emanu-El

Pacific Heights to Telegraph Hill

An infamous prison, a soaring monument and a former army barracks rise up in the northern section of the city. Also here are the roots of the Beat Generation and their antithesis: high-end shopping and sprawling homes in Pacific Heights.

Morning

Hop on an early ferry to **Alcatraz** (▷ 14–15), formerly an island prison and now one of San Francisco's most popular tourist destinations (reserve ahead, especially in summer). After a scenic ferry ride, you can tour the prison at your own pace accompanied by an audio tour, with commentary from former guards and inmates.

Mid-Morning

After you return from Alcatraz, explore **Pier 39** (▷ 126) and **Ghirardelli Square** (▷ 69), a chocolate factory that was converted into a complex of shops and restaurants in Fisherman's Wharf. Nearby, San Francisco's maritime history is well-documented at **Hyde Street Pier** (▷ 44–45), with its grand historical ships, some of which date as far back as the late 1800s.

Lunch

From Fisherman's Wharf it's a short drive or bus ride to **Chestnut Street** (▷ 67), which has a number of casual options for lunch. Consider flavorful tacos and ceviche at **Tacolicious** (▷ 149) or all-American burgers and fries at **Barney's Gourmet Hamburgers** (▷ 142), which has an enticing patio at the back.

Afternoon
Walk off lunch by window-shopping on Chestnut Street or by strolling along the **Marina Green** (▷ 71), where you can take in views of Alcatraz, Angel Island and the Golden Gate Bridge—and even fly a kite.

Mid-Afternoon
Then head back to Chestnut Street and take the 30 bus toward downtown; the bus will take you straight to the Italian neighborhood of **North Beach** (▷ 72). Walk through Washington Square Park en route to steep **Telegraph Hill** (▷ 24–25). Tackle the hill on foot or take bus 39 to reach **Coit Tower** (▷ 24–25), perched at the summit. The fluted concrete column has an observation gallery, but the views from Pioneer Park, at the base of the tower, are also incredible. After you return to North Beach, don't miss **City Lights** (▷ 123), a bookstore that was pivotal to the 1950s Beat Generation.

Dinner
There are a number of dinner options, whether you want Italian fare in North Beach or French, Asian or other cuisines on Union or Chestnut streets. New-American fare at **Gary Danko** (▷ 144), on the edge of Fisherman's Wharf, is expensive but worth it.

Evening
The after-dark choices here are plentiful, including live music, comedy, movie theaters and crowded bars (often skewing on the younger side). Consider getting tickets for Beach Blanket Babylon, a show that has run for decades at **Club Fugazi** (▷ 134). For laughs, there's always great improvisation at **BATS Improv** (▷ 133) in Fort Mason.

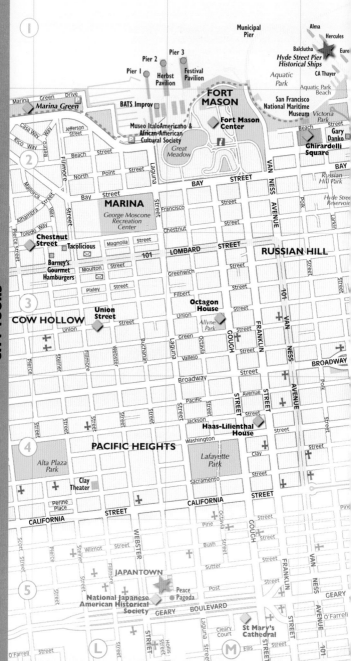

Municipal Pier

Alma
Hercules
Balclutha
Eure
Hyde Street Pier Historical Ships
CA Thayer

Pier 3
Pier 2
Festival Pavilion
Herbst Pavilion
Pier I

Aquatic Park
Aquatic Park Beach

Marina Green Drive
Marina Green

BATS Improv

FORT MASON

San Francisco National Maritime Museum

Fort Mason Center

Victoria Park

Beach Street
Gary Danko

Ghirardelli Square

Jefferson Street
Museo ItaloAmericano & African-American Cultural Society

Great Meadow

BAY

Casa Way
Rico Way
Buena Way

Beach Street
North Point Street
Street

Mallorca Street
Alhambra Street
Toledo Way
Pierce Street

BAY STREET

Russian Hill Park

Hyde Stree Reservoir

Polk
Larkin

VAN NESS AVENUE

Bay Street
MARINA
George Moscone Recreation Center

Francisco
Street

Chestnut Street

Chestnut Street

Magnolia Street
Tacolicious

Barney's Gourmet Hamburgers

Moulton Street

Pixley Street

101

LOMBARD STREET

Greenwich Street

Filbert Street

RUSSIAN HILL

Street

101

COW HOLLOW

Union Street

Union Street

Street

Octagon House

Union Street
Allyne Park
Green Street
Vallejo

GOUGH
FRANKLIN
VAN NESS

BROADWAY

Broadway

Street

Pacific Avenue

Jackson Street

Haas-Lilienthal House

STREET
Polk

PACIFIC HEIGHTS

Alta Plaza Park

Clay Theater

Washington
Clay Street

Lafayette Park

Sacramento

Perine Place

CALIFORNIA STREET

CALIFORNIA STREET

Pine Street

Bush Street

GOUGH
FRANKLIN
VAN NESS AVENUE

Scott Street
Pierce Street
Steiner Street
Wilmot Street
Fillmore Street
WEBSTER STREET

Sutter Street

JAPANTOWN

Post Street

National Japanese American Historical Society

Peace Pagoda

GEARY BOULEVARD

GEARY
O'Farrell

Laguna Street
Cleary Court

St Mary's Cathedral

Street

O'Farrell Street

Hollis Street

Ellis Street

101

L

M

90

Alcatraz,
Angel Island State Park

Pier 45
SS Jeremiah O'Brien
Ferry Dock
USS Pampanito
Pier 43
Pier 41
Pier 39
Complex
Fisherman's
Wharf
Pier 43.5
Pier 35
Cruise Ship
Terminal
Pier 33

Pier 47
The Embarcadero
Wax
Museum
Jefferson Street
Guiness
Museum
Ripleys
Museum
he
Cannery
Beach
Powell
Street
Stockton
Street
Kearny
Pier 31
Museum of the
City of San Francisco
TAYLOR
Mason
STREET
BAY
STREET
Montgomery
THE
Pier 29
NORTH
POINT
Pier 27
STREET
COLUMBUS
Francisco
Street
Chestnut
Street
Chestnut
Street
Lombard
Street
Lombard
Street
EMBARCADERO
Diego Rivera
Gallery
AVENUE
Coit
Tower
Pioneer
Park
Levi's
Plaza
Lombard
Street
Church of Saints
Peter and Paul
NORTH
BEACH
Washington
Square
Filbert
Street
TELEGRAPH
HILL
Filbert Street
Sansome
Greenwich
Street
Taylor
Street
Filbert
Street
Union
Street
Union Street
Battery
Street
Club Fugazi
Green
Street
NORTHEAST
WATERFRONT
HISTORIC DISTRICT
Ina
Coolbrith
Park
Vallejo
Street
Powell
Street
COLUMBUS
Vallejo
STREET
City Lights
AVENUE
BROADWAY
STREET
STREET
Pacific
Pacific
Street
CITY TOURS
Jackson
Street
Chinese
Culture
Center
Transamerica
Redwood Park
Cable Car
Museum
Washington
Street
CHINATOWN
Chinese Historical
Society of America
Pacific
Heritage
Museum
Transamerica
Pyramid
FINANCIAL
DISTRICT
NOB HILL
Clay
Street
Old
St Mary's
Cathedral
Wells Fargo
Museum
Sacramento
Huntington
Park
Fairmont
Hotel
555
California
Street
Pacific Coast
Stock Exchange
CALIFORNIA
Grace
Cathedral
STREET
Pine
Street
MARKET STREET
Bush
Street
Sutter
Street
Maiden
Lane
Montgomery
Street
New
0   500 m
0   500 yds
Union
Square
Maiden
Lane
STREET
GEARY
Museum of the African
Diaspora (MoAD)
Post
Street
Glide Memorial
Church
O'Farrell
Street
Contemporary
Jewish Museum
Macaulay
Park
Ellis
Street
Westfield
San Francisco
Center
San Francisco
Museum of
Modern Art
Yerba Buena
Gardens
Moscone
Convention
Center
Eddy
Street
Powell Street
Cartoon Art
Museum
MISSION
TENDERLOIN

Pacific Heights to Telegraph Hill
Quick Reference Guide

Alcatraz (▷ 14)

For nearly 30 years, "The Rock" was a top-security penitentiary and the country's most feared place of incarceration. Today the former island prison is a popular tourist draw with a colorful history, and the subject of many movies. Visitors can see former cells, the hospital, exercise yard and mess hall, as well as a museum explaining the wider history of the infamous island.

Coit Tower and Telegraph Hill (▷ 24)

A monument perched atop one of San Francisco's famous hills, the 180ft-high (55m) Coit Tower is visible from many parts of the city. Don't miss the 19 frescoed murals inside, or the views from the Observation Gallery, accessible by elevator. The tower, completed in 1933, was built thanks to a bequest from San Francisco socialite Lillie Hitchcock Coit.

Hyde Street Pier Historical Ships (▷ 44)

Though the city's seafaring heyday is in the past, the vessels docked at Hyde Street Pier serve as an engaging reminder of San Francisco's maritime roots. The most impressive ship is the *Balclutha*, dating from 1886, which rounded Cape Horn no less than 17 times. A World War II submarine is nearby at Pier 45.

CITY TOURS

Downtown to Nob Hill

Downtown is the city's hub for business and shopping, alongside the South of Market (SoMa) district, a first-rate destination for art and culture. Chinatown offers quirky shops and inexpensive food, while Nob Hill retains an elegance of the railroad tycoons who once lived here.

Morning
Start your day with a peek inside **Grace Cathedral** (▷ 42–43), noted for its stained glass, its playful labyrinths and its echoes of France's Notre-Dame. Outside the cathedral, stroll around **Nob Hill** (▷ 72) and relax in Huntington Park before making your way to the **Cable Car Museum** (▷ 16–17), where you can learn more about the charming (and slow!) mode of transportation that's unique to San Francisco.

Mid-Morning
Head down Washington Street toward **Chinatown** (▷ 67), exploring the quirky trinket shops on Grant Avenue. Then return to Washington, continuing east until you spot the **Transamerica Pyramid** (▷ 58–59), a distinctive part of the San Francisco skyline. Unfortunately, the building is no longer open to the general public, so your stop here will be quick. Then stroll around downtown, including a walk down pedestrian-only **Maiden Lane** (▷ 71) to check out the high-end boutiques and galleries; don't miss **Xanadu Gallery** (▷ 127), a Frank Lloyd Wright-designed building.

Lunch
For a casual, reasonably priced lunch, stop by the food court downstairs at the **Westfield San Francisco** center (▷ 127)—the quality is much better and varied than your average mall food court. After lunch, indulge in more shopping in the mall, which is anchored by Bloomingdales and Nordstrom department stores.

Afternoon

Don't miss the **San Francisco Museum of Modern Art** (▷ 56–57), in the SoMa district. The building itself is striking, and the ever-expanding permanent collection features 20th-century painting and sculpture, along with excellent photography. The **Museumstore** (▷ 125) is a great spot to find unusual gift items, while SFMOMA's cafés—one is on the ground floor and the other is part of the rooftop garden—serve savory and sweet treats.

Mid-Afternoon

There are a number of other museums in this area—too many to tackle in one afternoon. Depending on your interests, consider the **Cartoon Art Museum** (▷ 66), the **Museum of the African Diaspora** (MoAD; ▷ 72), the **Contemporary Jewish Museum** (▷ 28–29) or the galleries at **Yerba Buena Gardens** (▷ 62–63).

Early evening

After an afternoon of indoor culture, make a beeline for the **Embarcadero** (▷ 34–35). A walk along the water-front offers views of the Bay Bridge and outdoor sculpture. The **Ferry Building** (▷ 34–35), with its clock tower and vaulted ceiling, is architec-turally interesting.

Dinner

These neighborhoods offer a range of cuisines and prices, from inex-pensive Pakistani fare to high-end French food to authentic Chinese. Or you could sample American comfort food at **Wayfare Tavern** (▷ 149). After dinner, have a first-rate cocktail at **Bourbon & Branch** (▷ 133), a former speakeasy; you need to make a reservation online to get the password to enter. Or find out what's on at the respected **American Conservatory Theater** (▷ 132).

Lombard Street

Church of Saints Peter and Paul

NORTH BEACH

Coit Tower

TELEGRAPH HILL

Greenwich Street

Filbert Street

Union Street

Washington Square

Green Street

Hyde Street

Leavenworth Street

Jones Street

Taylor Street

Mason Street

Powell Street

Stockton Street

Columbus Avenue

Montgomery Street

Kearny Street

Iris Coolbrith Park

Union Street

Green Street

Vallejo Street

BROADWAY STREET

Pacific Avenue

Pacific Avenue

CHINATOWN

Chinese Culture Center

Transameric Pyrami

Jackson Street

Cable Car Museum

NOB HILL

Chinese Historical Society of America

Pacific Heritage Museum

Wayfare Tavern

Washington Street

Clay Street

Old St Mary's Cathedral

Wells Fargo Museum

Sacramento Street

Larkin Street

Sacramento Street

Huntington Park

Fairmont Hotel

CALIFORNIA STREET

555 California Street

Grace Cathedral

CALIFORNIA STREET

Pine Street

Bush Street

MONTGOMERY STREET

Pine Street

Sutter Street

Bush Street

Sutter Street

Post Street

Montgomery Street

Maiden Lane

Xanadu Gallery

Union Square

Maiden Lane

STREET

GEARY STREET

American Conservatory Theater

Museum of the African Diaspora (MoAD)

Post Street

O'Farrell Street

Bourbon & Branch

O'Farrell Street

Contemporary Jewish Museum

MISSION

Glide Memorial Church

Ellis Street

Westfield San Francisco Center

Yerba Buena Gardens

4TH STREET

STREET

TENDERLOIN

Eddy Street

Powell Street

Cartoon Art Museum

Turk Street

Moscone Center (West)

Children's Creativity Museum

5TH

Golden Gate Avenue

Pioneer Museum

Federal Building

State Building

McAllister Street

6TH STREET

HOWARD STREET

Asian Art Museum

City Hall

Library

Federal Building

7TH STREET

SOUTH OF MARKET

GROVE STREET

Civic Center

South of Market Park

Gramham Civic Auditorium

Hayes Street

8TH STREET

9TH STREET

MARKET

MISSION

HOWARD STREET

Hall of Justice

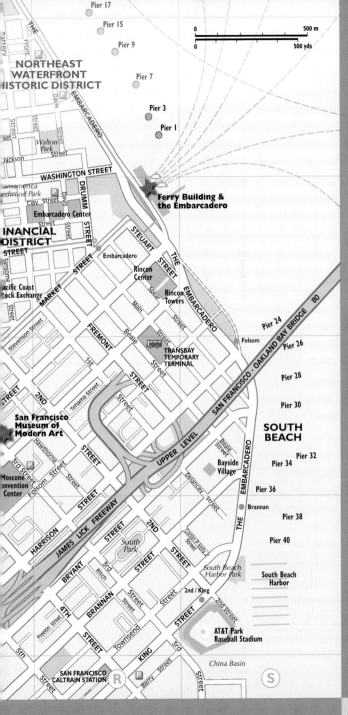

Pier 17

Pier 15

Pier 9

0   500 m

0   500 yds

Pier 7

NORTHEAST
WATERFRONT
HISTORIC DISTRICT

Davis   Street

Street

Pier 3

Pier 1

Walton
Park

Jackson   Street

WASHINGTON STREET

ansamerica
edwood Park

Clay   Street

DRUMM   STREET

Davis

**Ferry Building &
the Embarcadero**

Embarcadero Center

FINANCIAL
DISTRICT

Sansome

STREET

MARKET   STREET

STEUART   STREET

Embarcadero

Rincon
Center

Spear   Street

THE   EMBARCADERO

acific Coast
tock Exchange

Stevenson street

FREMONT   STREET

Main   Street

Beale   Street

Rincon
Towers

Pier 24

Folsom

Pier 26

CITY TOURS

TRANSBAY
TEMPORARY
TERMINAL

SAN FRANCISCO – OAKLAND BAY BRIDGE

80

STREET

2ND

1st   Street

Tehama   Street

STREET

Pier 28

Pier 30

**San Francisco
Museum of
Modern Art**

Hawthorne   Street

UPPER   LEVEL

Beale   Street

**SOUTH
BEACH**

Pier 32

Moscone
onvention
Center

Folsom   Street

STREET

**Bayside
Village**

Delancey   street

THE   EMBARCADERO

Pier 34

Pier 36

HARRISON   STREET

JAMES   LICK   FREEWAY

2ND   STREET

Colin P Kelly Jr

Brannan

Pier 38

BRYANT   STREET

South
Park

3rd   Street

STREET

Pier 40

3rd Street

BRANNAN   STREET

Ritch   Street

STREET

South Beach
Harbor Park

2nd / King

**South Beach
Harbor**

4TH   STREET

Freelon   street

STREET

Townsend   Street

KING   STREET

3rd   Street

2nd Street

**AT&T Park
Baseball Stadium**

5th

**SAN FRANCISCO
CALTRAIN STATION**

R

Berry   Street

P

China Basin

S

Downtown to Nob Hill
Quick Reference Guide

TOP 25 SIGHTS AND EXPERIENCES

MORE TO SEE   64

CITY TOURS

CITY TOURS

Western Addition to the Mission

Explore beyond San Francisco's high-profile sights and you'll be rewarded in these neighborhoods; home to diverse cultures, eye-catching murals, a beaux-arts masterpiece, a vast collection of Asian art and contrasts in places of worship.

Morning
Start the day in **Japantown** (▷ 46–47) exploring the Japan Center (▷ 124–125)—stores here sell everything from hard-to-find Japanese food to books and samurai swords. Then stop by the **National Japanese American Historical Society** (▷ 72), which features exhibits relating to the Japanese-American experience, and take a look at several churches in the area that are significant for their Japanese-style architecture.

Mid-Morning
Wander into the Civic Center's most beautiful building: the French baroque-styled **City Hall** (▷ 22–23). Tours are offered several times a day, but you can also ascend the grand staircase on your own and look around. Nearby is the **Asian Art Museum** (▷ 66), which has an immense collection spanning 6,000 years and diverse cultures and religions.

Lunch
From the Civic Center area it's a short walk over to **Hayes Valley** (▷ 70), a neighborhood that has undergone a transformation in the last two decades. Hayes Street, the main artery, is lined with interesting shops and restaurants—you can find casual cafés, burgers, pizza and more. **La Boulange de Hayes**, an outpost of La Boulange, a chain of popular French boulangeries, serves sandwiches, salads, brunch items and pastries (500 Hayes Street; daily 7–7).

Afternoon

Walk to **Alamo Square** (▷ 66) from the Hayes Valley shopping area, though be warned that the hill requires a bit of energy. You'll be rewarded at the top with the view of six famous Victorian homes known as the "painted ladies." You can also see the dome of City Hall, the Transamerica Pyramid and other sights from this perch.

Mid-Afternoon

Spend the rest of the afternoon in the **Mission District** (▷ 71–72), where you can explore the **Mission Dolores** (▷ 50–51), an adobe building completed in 1791. Mass is still held in the chapel, and also in the neighboring basilica, completed in 1918. Balmy Alley, between 24th and 25th streets, has the area's best murals. For a tour of these and other murals in the area, contact Precita Eyes Mural Center (▷ 71–72).

Dinner

The Mission is one of the best restaurant neighborhoods in the city. You won't be disappointed with the Italian fare at **Delfina** (▷ 144), but you're also unlikely to go wrong if you stumble on a place that looks busy and inviting. The neighborhood accommodates all price points and ethnic hankerings.

Evening

Nightlife is also lively in the Mission, where there's live music, clubs and countless bars, or you can see who's performing at **The Independent** (▷ 135), in the Western Addition. For cultural activities like the ballet, symphony and opera—held at Civic Center venues like **Louise M. Davies Symphony Hall** (▷ 135) and the **War Memorial Opera House** (▷ 137)—you'll have to plan ahead and buy tickets in advance.

+ JAPANTOWN

Sutter Street
Post Street

National Japanese
American Historical
Society

Peace
Pagoda

GEARY BOULEVARD

St Mary's
Cathedral

Cleary
Court

Ellis

O'Farrell Street

Jefferson
Square

St John Coltrane
African Orthodox
Church

Eddy
Turk

ANZA VISTA

Golden Gate

Turk
McAllister

Golden Gate Avenue

VAN NESS
CIVIC CENTER

WESTERN
ADDITION

Fulton

African American
Art & Culture
Complex

Octavia
Grove
Ivy Street

Alamo
Square

HAYES VALLEY

La Boulange
de Hayes

The Independent

Hayes Street

ALAMO SQUARE

FELL STREET

Hickory

FELL
Street
OAK

OAK STREET

Page

Koshland
Park

Haight

Page Street

Waller Street

Haight Street

Waller

Hermann Street

Buena
Vista
Park

Duboce
Park

Duboce
Park

Pearl
Street

DUBOCE

Duboce Avenue

Duboce /
Church

14th Street

Corona
Heights
Park

CASTRO

14th Street
Henry Street

Church Street

GUERRERO

Randall
Museum

15th Street

15th Street

Beaver Street

MISSION DOLORES

Museum Way

States Street

16TH STREET

Mission
Dolores

DOLORES

17TH STREET

Castro

17th Street

Ford Street

Church

MARKET STREET

CASTRO

18th Street

18TH STREET

Hancock Street

Church /
18th

Delfina

Dolores
Park

19th Street

Broderick
DIVISADERO
SCOTT
Pierce Street
Steiner
Fillmore
Webster
Hollis Street
Laguna
Buchanan
Mall

102

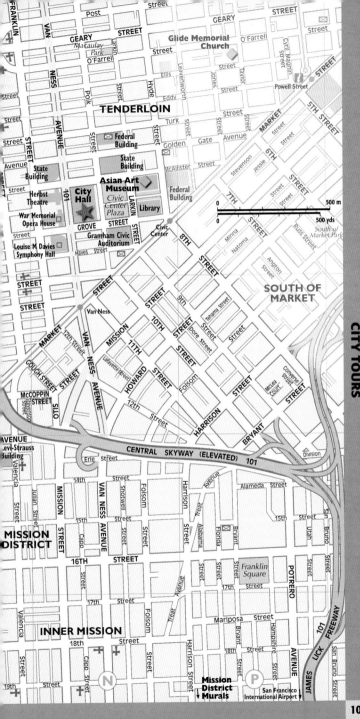

FRANKLIN

Post Street

VAN NESS

GEARY STREET

GEARY STREET
Macaulay Park
O'Farrell

Glide Memorial Church

O'Farrell Street

Cyril Magnin Street

STREET

Street

Street

Larkin Street

Ellis Street

Jones Street

Taylor Street

Leavenworth Street

Hyde Street

Polk Street

Eddy Street

Powell Street

5TH STREET

TENDERLOIN

Turk Street

Golden Gate Avenue

MARKET

Street

NESS AVENUE

State Building

Federal Building

State Building

McAllister Street

6TH STREET

7TH STREET

Street

Herbst Theatre

City Hall

Asian Art Museum

Civic Center Plaza

Library

Federal Building

Stevenson

Jessie Street

Street

War Memorial Opera House

GROVE STREET

LARKIN

0   500 m

Louise M Davies Symphony Hall

Gramham Civic Auditorium

Hayes Street

Civic Center

8TH STREET

0   500 yds

Russ Street

South of Market Park

STREET

Minna Street

Natoma Street

SOUTH OF MARKET

STREET

Van Ness

MARKET

12th Street

VAN NESS AVENUE

MISSION

10TH STREET

9TH STREET

STREET

Tehama Street

Dore Street

Street

Angton Street

STREET

11TH STREET

HOWARD STREET

Lafayette Street

FOLSOM

Converse Street

STREET

McLea Court

COUGH STREET

SILO

12th Street

HARRISON

BRYANT

McCoppin Street

Stevenson Street

AVENUE
Levi-Strauss Building

Valencia

CENTRAL SKYWAY (ELEVATED) 101

Division

Erie Street

14th Street

MISSION

VAN NESS AVENUE

Shotwell Street

Folsom Street

Harrison Street

Treat Avenue

Alameda Street

San Bruno

101 LICK FREEWAY

Julian Street

15th Street

Capp Street

Street

Alabama Street

Florida Street

Bryant Street

15th Street

Utah Street

MISSION DISTRICT

STREET

16TH STREET

Franklin Square

POTRERO

Street

17th Street

Mariposa Street

JAMES LICK FREEWAY

Valencia

17th Street

INNER MISSION

18th Street

Folsom Street

Treat Avenue

Harrison Street

Bryant Street

18th Street

Hampshire Street

AVENUE

San Bruno Avenue

Street

Capp Street

19th Street

Street

Mission District Murals

San Francisco International Airport

Western Addition to the Mission
Quick Reference Guide

City Hall (▷ 22)

This beaux-arts masterpiece has a black-and-gold copper dome that can be seen from many points around the city. Inside, the grand staircase is lined with wrought-iron banisters and illuminated by free-standing and hanging lamps. The building was completed in 1915 at a cost of $3.5 million. The aim of the authorities was to show San Francisco's superiority over the city of Los Angeles.

Japantown (▷ 46)

San Francisco's Japanese-American community, the first in the United States, once spanned 30 blocks of the Western Addition. Today Japantown's commercial hub is the large Japan Center (two indoor malls connected by a plaza), while several churches in the area feature Japanese-style architecture. Other highlights include the National Japanese American Historical Society.

Mission Dolores (▷ 50)

Part of a chain of 21 missions built in California by the Spanish, Mission Dolores is the oldest building in the city. Its thick adobe walls helped the structure withstand several earthquakes. Headstones in the cemetery mark Spanish- and Mexican-era notables. The mission's tiny yet atmospheric chapel has an altar dating from 1780, as well as frescoes by Native Americans.

Golden Gate Park

One of the world's largest urban parks, Golden Gate Park stretches from the middle of the city to the ocean, encompassing outstanding museums, gardens, lakes, a golf course and windmills. Nearby is the freethinking Haight-Ashbury, birthplace of 1967's Summer of Love.

Morning

You could spend all day walking around **Golden Gate Park** (▷ 40–41), but start your exploration at one of a trio of lovely gardens, all located in the eastern section of the park: the **Conservatory of Flowers** (▷ 68), the **Japanese Tea Garden** (▷ 70–71) and the **San Francisco Botanical Garden at Strybing Arboretum** (▷ 74). Nature lovers will appreciate the incredible variety of plants and flowers on view from around the globe at any one of these sights.

Mid-Morning

Two very different but impressive museums are just a short walk from each other, so choose which one you'd like to visit: The **de Young** (▷ 30–31) is an art museum that also plays host to first-rate traveling exhibitions; the **California Academy of Sciences** (▷ 18–19) covers everything from the land and sea to the outer reaches of the solar system; there are a number of exhibits and activities that will entertain children, including the state-of-the-art Morrison Planetarium.

Lunch

Both museums have solid dining choices, so stick around for lunch. The **de Young's café** has outdoor seating by its sculpture garden, while the California Academy of Sciences has highly regarded chefs behind its restaurant (**Moss Room**) and its more casual **café**.

Afternoon

Explore more of **Golden Gate Park**. Activities include a boat ride on Stow Lake and a carousel ride for kids, or take advantage of one of the park's 21 tennis courts (lessons are available, too). Then take a short detour north of the park to explore the **Columbarium** (▷ 26–27), a Victorian structure that houses ashes of the deceased. While it might sound morbid, it's quintessentially San Francisco (though many locals don't even know it exists). Arrange a tour, if possible—almost every niche has a fascinating story.

Mid-Afternoon

Wander down historic Haight Street, in **Haight-Ashbury** (▷ 70). The area's hippie, Summer-of-Love reputation has shifted over the years and yuppies might now trump deadheads (followers of the band the Grateful Dead). But the area still bears some vestiges of its Grateful Dead roots, with shops selling tie-dye shirts, pipes and other deadhead gear. Other stores sell funky, contemporary clothes and shoes.

Dinner

Stay in the Haight-Ashbury area for dinner and nightlife. At a spot like **Alembic** (▷ 132), you can have both in one location. After dinner, find out what's playing at the **Red Vic** (1727 Haight Street), an independent movie theater showing a mix of recent and old films. Note that it's wise to steer clear of Golden Gate Park after dark—as with any park, there are many isolated areas that aren't safe at night.

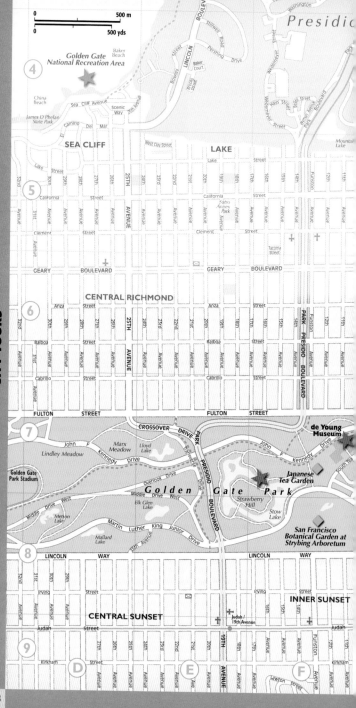

0 | 500 m
0 | 500 yds

④ Golden Gate
National Recreation Area

Baker Beach

China Beach

Sea Cliff Avenue

James D Phelan State Park

Camino Del Mar

Scenic Way

SEA CLIFF

West Clay Street

LAKE

Lake Street

Lake Street

Bowley Street

LINCOLN Boulevard

Baker Court

Pershing Drive

Stilwell Road

Compton Row

Washington Boulevard

Boulevard

Presidio

Wedemeyer Street

Upton Street

Mays Street

Storey Avenue

Ruger Street

Park Boulevard

Mountain Lake

⑤ California Street

California Street

Clement Street

Clement Street

Sutro Annes Park

Tacoma Street

32nd Avenue | 31st Avenue | 30th Avenue | 29th Avenue | 28th Avenue | 27th Avenue | 26th Avenue | 25TH AVENUE | 24th Avenue | 23rd Avenue | 22nd Avenue | 21st Avenue | 20th Avenue | 19th Avenue | 18th Avenue | 17th Avenue | 16th Avenue | 15th Avenue | 14th Avenue | Funston Avenue | 12th Avenue | 11th Avenue

GEARY BOULEVARD

GEARY BOULEVARD

⑥ **CENTRAL RICHMOND**

Anza Street

Anza Street

Balboa Street

Balboa Street

Cabrillo Street

Cabrillo Street

PARK PRESIDIO BOULEVARD

FULTON STREET

FULTON STREET

⑦ CROSSOVER DRIVE

PARK

de Young Museum

John F Kennedy Drive

Marx Meadow

Lloyd Lake

John F Kennedy Drive

Lindley Meadow

Golden Gate Park Stadium

Overlook Drive

Golden Gate Park

Middle Drive West

Elk Glen Lake

Japanese Tea Garden

Strawberry Hill

South Tea

Stow Lake

PRESIDIO DRIVE

BOULEVARD

Metson Lake

Middle Drive West

Martin Luther King Junior Drive

Mallard Lake

35th Avenue

San Francisco Botanical Garden at Strybing Arboretum

⑧ **LINCOLN WAY**

LINCOLN WAY

Irving Street

Irving Street

INNER SUNSET

CENTRAL SUNSET

Judah Street

Judah / 19th Avenue

Judah Street

⑨ Kirkham Street

Kirkham Street

Lawton Street

32nd Avenue | 31st Avenue | 30th Avenue | 29th Avenue | 28th Avenue | 27th Avenue | 26th Avenue | 25th Avenue | 24th Avenue | 23rd Avenue | 22nd Avenue | 21st Avenue | 20th Avenue | 19TH AVENUE | 18th Avenue | 17th Avenue | 16th Avenue | 15th Avenue | 14th Avenue | Funston Avenue | 12th Avenue | 11th Avenue

D | **E** | **F**

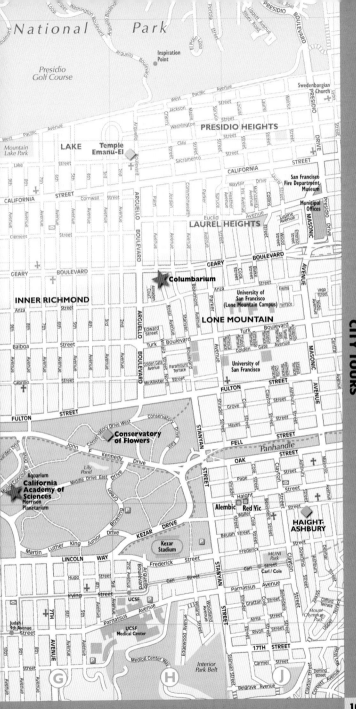

SIGHTS AND EXPERIENCES

CITY TOURS

California Academy of Sciences (▷ 18)

Pritzker Prize-winning architect Renzo Piano designed this "green" museum, creating a living roof that houses a state-of-the-art planetarium, an aquarium, natural history museum and rainforest dome, where the temperature reaches a warming 85°F (29°C).

Columbarium (▷ 26)

This four-story Victorian rotunda, which opened in 1898, is a final resting place for urns holding the ashes of the deceased. Eddys, Turks and other once-illustrious families have niches here, and there's a memorial to gay-rights activist Harvey Milk, who was assassinated in 1978.

de Young Museum (▷ 30)

Damage to the de Young Museum from the 1989 Loma Prieta earthquake led to a stunning new building in Golden Gate Park, unveiled in 2005. The permanent collection focuses on American painting and decorative arts; the 144ft (44m) observation tower is a highlight.

Golden Gate Park (▷ 40)

Modeled after New York's Central Park, this vast, 1,000-acre (405ha) urban park is home to museums, gardens, lakes, windmills, a golf course and more; it also hosts festivals and special events throughout the year and it's popular with joggers, kite-fliers and roller-skaters.

MORE TO SEE 64

ENTERTAINMENT 128

EAT 138

CITY TOURS

Eye-catching decoration on a house in Haight-Ashbury

Enjoying the Japanese Tea Garden

Further Afield

If you have a bit more time in the Bay Area, explore a few neighborhoods and state parks that are slightly off the tourist path, but worth investigating. Also incorporate a trip across the Bay Bridge to Berkeley and Oakland, where the weather warms up and the fog lifts, but the character remains.

DAY 1
Morning
Spend your morning in the East Bay, starting with the **UC Berkeley Campus** (▷ 60–61). Amble down Telegraph Avenue, the main drag on the south side of campus, and walk through Sather Gate to see Sproul Plaza, where the 1960s Free Speech Movement was born. The Campanile is also a highlight.

Lunch
Don't miss the opportunity to try **Chez Panisse** café (1517 Shattuck Avenue, Berkeley; Mon–Sat), helmed by influential chef Alice Waters, who has been a proponent of local, seasonal ingredients for decades. Her formal restaurant downstairs is open for dinner only, but her upstairs café is less expensive and open for lunch.

Afternoon
After lunch, visit the **Oakland Museum of California** (▷ 52–53), which provides lively, informative exhibits about the ever-evolving art, history and nature of California. Its garden has lovely views of Lake Merritt.

Dinner
Go to the Berkeley/Oakland border to dine at **Wood Tavern** (6317 College Avenue, Oakland; daily lunch and dinner), a neighborhood restaurant serving California-Mediterranean cuisine on College Avenue. The street also has other good dining options, a movie theater, cafés and bars.

DAY 2
Morning
Start your day exploring two side-by-side neighborhoods with different personalities: **Noe Valley** (▷ 75) and the **Castro** (▷ 75). The heart of commercial Noe Valley is 24th Street, where you'll share the sidewalk with strollers (pushchairs) and dogs as you peruse the inviting shops. Then head over to the Castro, San Francisco's famous gay district, where politician and gay-rights activist Harvey Milk opened his camera shop and launched a movement. Most of the action is on Castro Street between Market and 19th streets; the famous **Castro Theatre** (▷ 133) is on Castro and Market.

Lunch
Make your way across town to the **Fort Mason Center** (▷ 68–69) and **Greens** (▷ 144–145), a vegetarian restaurant where even meat-lovers won't miss a thing, especially with the views of the Golden Gate Bridge and the San Francisco Bay.

Afternoon
From Fort Mason, walk over to Fisherman's Wharf and take a scenic ferry ride to **Angel Island State Park** (▷ 75), which is the largest island in the Bay (though not as famous as Alcatraz, its neighbor). Angel Island has hiking trails and bike paths to keep you occupied for several hours.

Evening
Take the ferry back to Fisherman's Wharf and ride the cable car up steep Hyde Street to **Zarzuela** (▷ 149), a Russian Hill restaurant serving tapas, sangria and other traditional Spanish dishes. After dinner, walk down to Polk Street for a nightcap.

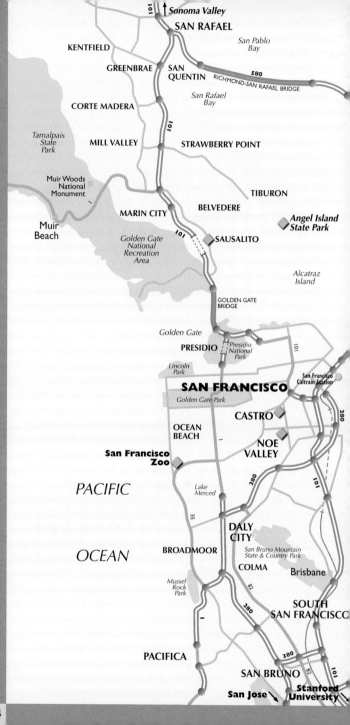

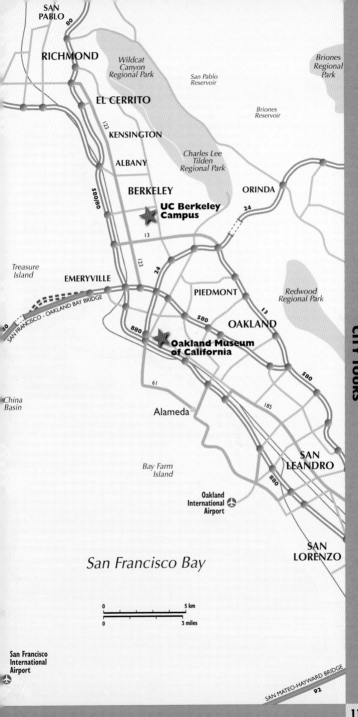

SAN
PABLO

80

RICHMOND

*Wildcat
Canyon
Regional Park*

*San Pablo
Reservoir*

*Briones
Regional
Park*

EL CERRITO

123

KENSINGTON

*Briones
Reservoir*

ALBANY

*Charles Lee
Tilden
Regional Park*

580|80

BERKELEY

ORINDA

24

**UC Berkeley
Campus**

13

123

24

*Treasure
Island*

EMERYVILLE

PIEDMONT

*Redwood
Regional
Park*

SAN FRANCISCO - OAKLAND BAY BRIDGE

13

80

880

580

OAKLAND

*China
Basin*

61

**Oakland Museum
of California**

580

185

Alameda

SAN
LEANDRO

*Bay Farm
Island*

880

Oakland
International
Airport

SAN
LORENZO

San Francisco Bay

0 _____ 5 km

0 _____ 3 miles

San Francisco
International
Airport

SAN MATEO-HAYWARD BRIDGE

92

Further Afield Quick Reference Guide

 SIGHTS AND EXPERIENCES

Oakland Museum of California (▷ 52)

This East Bay museum leads the way in documenting the history, nature and art of the Golden State. An extensive renovation, slated for completion by early 2012, has added a spring in the museum's step; it's now a much more interactive, entertaining place.

UC Berkeley Campus (▷ 60)

Museums, libraries and architecturally distinguished buildings draw visitors to this campus, once a hotbed of political dissent. The first of 10 University of California campuses, highlights for visitors include the Berkeley Art Museum, the elegant Sather Gate and the Campanile.

MORE TO SEE	64

Angel Island State Park	San Jose
Castro	Sausalito
Noe Valley	Sonoma Valley
San Francisco Zoo	Stanford University

SHOP	118

Clothes	**Offbeat**
Worn Out West	Global Exchange

ENTERTAINMENT	128

Bars and Cafés	**Movie Theaters**
Café Flore	Castro Theatre

EAT	138

Asian
Eric's Restaurant

Shop

Whether you're looking for the best local products, a department store or a quirky boutique, you'll find them all in San Francisco. In this section shops are listed alphabetically.

SHOP

Introduction

While San Francisco may not be in the same shopping league as London, Paris or New York, many prefer its slower pace and are surprised by the array of paraphernalia to be found. Each neighborhood reflects its style in the clothes, furnishings, antiques, books, food and souvenirs on offer, making shopping an enjoyable accompaniment to exploring these different areas.

A Memento of Your Visit

Various knick-knacks decorated with the Golden Gate Bridge, Alcatraz or the words "I Left My Heart in San Francisco" predominate among the souvenirs widely found in Fisherman's Wharf and the smaller sprinkling of trinket outlets in Chinatown and downtown. Those of a nervous disposition might choose to avoid the many jokey earthquake-related items, while Ghirardelli chocolate makes a good gift for anyone with a sweet tooth. The produce of California's numerous wineries is stocked throughout the city. Having chosen your wine, head to the local bakery for a loaf of Boudin's sourdough bread (▷ 143). The Boudin tradition continues with the same distinctive sourdough that arrived in San Francisco during the Gold Rush. A local specialty is fresh clam chowder served in a sourdough bread bowl.

Something Unique

In Chinatown and the less-tourist-visited Asian shops on Clement Street in the Richmond District are rich pickings for amateur cooks

Clockwise from top: Shop signs in Haight-Ashbury; food and drink at Molinari Deli, in the Italian District; bags for sale in a store in Fillmore Street; pink lilies

SHOP

looking to extend their stocks of utensils or to select from an array of otherwise hard-to-find spices and herbs.

Vintage San Francisco

Rich with new and secondhand bookstores, San Francisco was a fulcrum of the 1950s Beat explosion and is the best place to find the definitive stock of Beat and Beat-related literature and criticism. Haight-Ashbury's original hippies may have moved on but the tie-dyed T-shirts and other totems of flower power are still available along Haight Street, which is also the best stop in the city for wacky, vintage clothing and obscure CDs and vinyl.

Other Shopping Districts

Other noted neighborhood shopping streets include Chestnut Street in the Marina District, Union and Fillmore streets in Pacific Heights, and Hayes Street in burgeoning Hayes Valley, all proferring generally smart clothing, antiques and household items. In North Beach, Grant Avenue has outlets for bric-a-brac and unusual crafts as well as silks and pearls. The Mission District has become a destination for furniture, funky designers and independent stores.

STYLE OVER SUBSTANCE

"Design matters" proclaimed the San Francisco-based magazine *One*. The publication lasted less than a year, but the slogan is still relevant. Design has always played an important role in San Francisco. The iconic images of the Golden Gate National Recreation Area from graphic designer Michael Schweb are found on posters, mugs, T-shirts and calendars. Furniture is also an art form in some San Francisco stores. At Limn (✉ 290 Townsend Street ☎ 415/543–5466) check out contemporary pieces by European and European-influenced designers. New Deal (✉ 4529 18th Street ☎ 415/552–6208) has furniture, lighting and artworks to enhance any design-conscious pad.

make a cheerful greeting for customers; Californian wine is a popular purchase; loaves of sourdough bread and tins of Clam Chowder for sale at Boudin's Bakery

Directory

SHOP

Shopping A–Z

ANDREA SCHWARTZ GALLERY

www.asgallery.com
This large exhibition space is devoted to contemporary painting, installations and mixed media.
✚ R6 ✉ 525 2nd Street ☎ 415/495–2090 🕐 Mon–Fri 9–5, Sat 1–5
🚌 10, 30, 45

APPLE STORE

www.apple.com/retail/sanfrancisco
Where better to sample Apple's latest innovations? Expect product demos and a buzzing atmosphere.
✚ Q5 ✉ 1 Stockton Street ☎ 415/392–0202 🕐 Mon–Sat 9–9, Sun 10–8
🚌 2, 3, 30, 45

CHANEL BOUTIQUE

www.chanel.com

Two floors filled with clothes, cosmetics and much more from the renowned French designer are available for the woman with refined taste.

➕ Q5 ✉ 156 Geary Street ☎ 415/981–1550 ⏰ Mon–Sat 10–6, Sun 12–5
🚌 2, 3, 30, 45

CITY LIGHTS

www.citylights.com

City Lights is a publishing company and bookstore, inextricably linked to the 1950s Beat Generation, founded by poet Lawrence Ferlinghetti. The stock includes many of the movement's definitive writings, fiction and nonfiction, and literary magazines.

➕ Q3 ✉ 261 Columbus Avenue ☎ 415/362–8193 ⏰ Daily 10am–midnight
🚌 30, 41, 45

CLARION MUSIC CENTER

www.clarionmusic.com

Regulars might rent a violin or cello, but others can content themselves with a stroll along the racks browsing the wonderful Asian musical instruments, which range from Burmese temple bells to Chinese egg rattles.

➕ Q4 ✉ 816 Sacramento Street ☎ 415/391–1317 ⏰ Mon–Fri 11–6, Sat 9–5 🚌 30, 45

CRIS

Secondhand-clothes store Cris is a welcome surprise for budget-conscious shoppers in the usually expensive Russian Hill neighbor-hood, with an array of designer names; mostly for women, though there is a menswear section.

➕ N3 ✉ 2056 Polk Street ☎ 415/474–1191 ⏰ Mon–Sat 11–6, Sun 12–5 🚌 19

CROCKER GALLERIA

www.thecrockergalleria.com

Designer clothing stores, food shops and snack stands make this small, chic shopping mall in the Financial District ideal for browsing.

➕ Q5 ✉ 50 Post Street ☎ 415/393–1505 ⏰ Mon–Fri 10–6, Sat 10–5 🚌 2, 3, 5, 6

CROSSROADS TRADING CO.

www.crossroadstrading.com

Here you'll find secondhand and discounted new clothes and jewelry, with a youthful bias.

➕ L5 ✉ 1901 Fillmore Street ☎ 415/775–8885 ⏰ Mon–Thu 11–7, Fri–Sat 11–8, Sun 11–7 🚌 2, 3, 4, 22, 76

DEMA

www.godemago.com

Stylish stores line Valencia Street, including this shop, with women's designs from owner Dema Grim.

➕ M9 ✉ 1038 Valencia Street ☎ 415/206–0500 ⏰ Mon–Fri 11–7, Sat 12–7, Sun 12–6 🚇 24th Street–Mission 🚌 14, 49

COFFEE TO GO

The city's preponderance of cafés has helped make San Franciscans discerning coffee drink-ers. The expertise extends to the purchase of coffee for brewing at home, and the city has acquired several highly regarded outlets for what has been termed "gourmet coffee." One of the most popular is Peet's Coffee and Tea (✉ 2156 Chestnut Street; and at more than 20 locations across the city), which has been roasting and brewing coffee in the Bay Area since 1966 and stocks beans from around the coffee-growing world together with a formidable variety of grinders and espresso machines.

NEIMAN MARCUS

The opening of Neiman Marcus in Stockton Street in 1982 was met with a certain sadness by San Franciscans. Whatever their feelings for the store itself, they were generally not enamored of its postmodern design or the fact it replaced the City of Paris department store, built in 1896. The latter's glass rotunda was retained, however, and can be admired over tea in the Rotunda restaurant.

EMBARCADERO CENTER

www.embarcaderocenter.com

Pick up a free map to plot a course around the walkways, plazas and stores of this three-level shopping complex spanning eight city blocks.

➕ R4 ✉ Battery Street, between Clay and Sacramento streets ☎ 415/772–0700 🕐 Mon–Fri 10–7, Sat 10–6, Sun 12–5 🚌 1, 41

GHIRARDELLI SQUARE

▷ 69.

GIMME SHOES

www.gimmeshoes.com

This store sells shoes by a range of designers, from Sigerson Morrison to Adidas.

➕ L4 ✉ 2358 Fillmore Street ☎ 415/441–3040 🕐 Mon–Sat 11–7, Sun 12–6 🚌 1, 22

GLOBAL EXCHANGE

www.globalexchangestore.com

The store of a human rights organization sells clothing, artworks and more from the Third World, guaranteed not to be produced in sweatshops or in environmentally destructive ways.

➕ Off map at L9 ✉ 4018 24th Street ☎ 415/648–8068 🕐 Mon, Sun 11–6, Tue–Fri 11–7, Sat 10–7 🚇 16th Street–Mission 🚌 37, 48

GUMP'S

www.gumps.com

Gump's has been held in high esteem since 1861 and sells antiques from all over the world, particularly Asia. An art gallery specializes in works by emergent artists and another room is devoted to jade.

➕ Q5 ✉ 135 Post Street ☎ 415/982–1616 🕐 Mon–Sat 10–6, Sun 12–5 🚌 2, 3, 76

HANG ART

www.hangart.com

Hang Art displays what it believes is the cream of the new crop of Bay Area artists.

➕ P5 ✉ 567 Sutter Street ☎ 415/434–4264 🕐 Mon–Sat 10–6, Sun 12–5 🚌 1, 3, 38

HEIDI SAYS

www.heidisays.com

This Pacific Heights boutique has clothes, shoes and accessories from new and established designers. Heidi Says Casual is two doors down, and Heidi Says Shoes is down the street (2105 Fillmore).

➕ L4 ✉ 2426 Fillmore Street ☎ 415/749–0655 🕐 Mon–Sat 11–7, Sun 12–6 🚌 1, 22

THE HOUND

www.thehound.com

The Hound offers expensive, high-quality menswear, much of it based on popular perceptions of what an English country gentleman likes to wear.

➕ Q4 ✉ 140 Sutter Street ☎ 415/989–0429 🕐 Mon–Fri 9.30–6, Sat 9.30–5.30 🚌 2, 3, 76

JAPAN CENTER

From kimonos to rice cookers to samurai swords, Japanese arts and crafts are well represented in this complex of stores, restaurants and offices.

L5–M5 ✉ Post Street, between Laguna and Fillmore streets ☎ No phone ⏰ Store and restaurant hours vary 🚌 2, 3, 38

JEREMYS

www.jeremys.com

A wide selection of discounted men's and women's clothing is sold here, often from high-end designers and department stores. Be aware that some items have slight defects.

R6 ✉ 2 South Park ☎ 415/882–4929 ⏰ Mon–Wed, Fri–Sat 11–6, Thu 11–8, Sun 12–6 🚌 10

JOHN BERGGRUEN GALLERY

www.berggruen.com

Some of the leading names of 20th-century American art are to be found through the three floors of this highly regarded gallery, which also features selected European works.

Q5 ✉ 228 Grant Avenue ☎ 415/781–4629 ⏰ Mon–Fri 9.30–5.30, Sat 10.30–5 🚌 2, 3, 76

METIER

www.metiersf.com

This understated boutique just off Union Square carries a wide range of high-quality clothing, jewelry and accessories from the likes of Alexander Wang, 3.1 Phillip Lim and Vanessa Bruno.

Q5 ✉ 335 Sutter Street ☎ 415/989–5395 ⏰ Mon–Sat 10–6 🚌 3, 30, 45

MINGLE

www.mingleshop.com

Designers and artists rotate frequently at this boutique selling clothes, jewelry, accessories and art. New items, often one-of-a-kind, enter the mix weekly.

M3 ✉ 1815 Union Street ☎ 415/674–8811 ⏰ Wed–Mon 11–7 🚌 41, 45

MUSEUMSTORE

http://sfmoma.stores.yahoo.net

The store of the San Francisco Museum of Modern Art sells an exemplary collection of art-related books, posters and souvenirs.

Q5 ✉ San Francisco Museum of Modern Art, 151 3rd Street ☎ 888/357–0037 ⏰ Mon–Wed, Fri–Sun 10–6.30, Thu 10–9.30 🚌 12, 30, 45, 76

NATIONAL PARK STORE

http://store.parksconservancy.org/store

Browse here for books, magazines and videos devoted to wild California and the natural history of the American West.

P1 ✉ Pier 39, Fisherman's Wharf ☎ 415/433–7221 ⏰ Sun–Thu 10–9, Fri–Sat 10–9.30 🚌 10, 19, 47

ONE-STOP SHOPPING

Shoppers will discover many major department stores within walking distance of each other, either in the Union Square area or in Westfield San Francisco shopping center. Neiman Marcus (✉ 150 Stockton Street ☎ 415/362–3900), Saks Fifth Avenue (✉ 220 Post Street ☎ 415/986–4300), Bloomingdale's (✉ Westfield San Francisco, 865 Market Street ☎ 415/856–5720) and Barneys New York (✉ 77 O'Farrell Street ☎ 415/268–3500) compete for attention from bigger spenders, while Macy's West (✉ 170 O'Farrell Street ☎ 415/397–3333) and Nordstrom (✉ Westfield San Francisco, 865 Market Street ☎ 415/243–8500) have quality merchandise at more affordable prices.

NEEDLES & PENS
www.needles-pens.com
Needles & Pens sells clothes and other exclusive creations from local artists, plus a vast stock of off-beat magazines and local magazines published on a shoestring.
🔳 M8 ✉ 3252 16th Street ☎ 415/255–1534 🕐 Daily 12–7 🚇 16th Street–Mission 🚌 14, 49

OOMA
www.ooma.net
At Ooma ("objects of my affection") you'll find bright and breezy designer womenswear and accessories that range from polka-dot bikinis to flower-clad shoes.
🔳 Q3 ✉ 1422 Grant Avenue ☎ 415/627–6963 🕐 Tue–Sat 11–7, Sun 12–5 🚌 41, 45

PIER 39
www.pier39.com
With 100 or more stores to choose from, visitors to Pier 39 can find San Francisco souvenirs, magic kits, crazy hats and more. Don't miss the sunbathing sea lions.
🔳 P1 ✉ Pier 39, Fisherman's Wharf 🕐 Sun–Thu 10–9, Fri–Sat 10–10 (shorter hours in winter) 🚌 8X, 39, 47, F

There's plenty of choice at Pier 39

ROLO SOMA
www.rolo.com
Rolo designs take their inspiration from street fashion, conjuring up extrovert attire for the daring man or woman who wishes to appear hip on the social circuit.
🔳 P7 ✉ 1301 Howard Street ☎ 415/578–7139, ext. 100 🕐 Mon–Sat 11–7, Sun 12–6 🚌 12

SEPHORA
www.sephora.com
A visual explosion of color accompanies high-end cosmetics and fragrances from companies such as Stila and Christian Dior.
🔳 P5 ✉ 33 Powell Street ☎ 415/362–9360 🕐 Mon–Sat 10–9, Sun 10–7 🚇 Powell Street 🚌 30, 45

TEN REN TEA COMPANY
www.tenren.com
This Chinatown store is packed with more than 40 blends from around the world. You can taste before you buy.
🔳 Q4 ✉ 949 Grant Avenue ☎ 415/362–0656 🕐 Mon–Sat 9–9 🚌 30, 41

THRIFT TOWN
www.thrifttown.com
Packed from floor to ceiling with donated secondhand clothing, furniture, books and lots more, this is one of the largest of San Francisco's thrift stores. Many others are listed in the phone book.
🔳 N9 ✉ 2101 Mission Street ☎ 415/861–1132 🕐 Mon–Fri 9–8, Sat 10–7, Sun 10–6 🚇 16th Street–Mission 🚌 14, 49

VER UNICA
Ver Unica has a mighty stock of vintage wear, for both men and

women, plus shoes, handbags and assorted accessories.

🔒 M6 ✉ 437B Hayes Street ☎ 415/431–0688 🕐 Mon–Sat 11–7, Sun 10–6 🚌 21

WESTFIELD SAN FRANCISCO

http://westfield.com/sanfrancisco

Nordstrom and Bloomingdale's department stores anchor this large indoor shopping center.

🔒 Q5 ✉ 865 Market Street ☎ 415/512–6776 🕐 Mon–Sat 10–8.30, Sun 10–8 Ⓟ Powell Street 🚌 5, 6, 9, 21, 31, 71

WILKES BASHFORD

You'll find classy men's and women's clothing across six impressively well-stocked floors here.

🔒 Q4 ✉ 375 Sutter Street ☎ 415/986–4380 🕐 Mon–Sat 10–6 🚌 2, 3, 30, 45, 76

WILLIAM STOUT ARCHITECTURAL BOOKS

www.stoutbooks.com

Architectural tomes in sufficient quantity to attract both the professional architect and the interested amateur are stocked at this store.

🔒 Q3 ✉ 804 Montgomery Street ☎ 415/391–6757 🕐 Mon–Fri 10–6.30, Sat 10–5.30 🚌 41

WORN OUT WEST

www.wornoutwest.com

What started out fulfilling the sartorial needs of gay men in pursuit of the cowboy look has evolved into a cornucopia of high-quality used western wear, from Stetson hats and snakeskin boots to exceptionally attractive bolo ties.

🔒 L9 ✉ 582 Castro Street ☎ 415/431–6020 🕐 Sun–Fri 12–7, Sat 11–7 🚌 24

SECONDHAND BOOKS

Recommended stores for used books include Borderlands Books (✉ 866 Valencia Street ☎ 415/824–8203), with science fiction and fantasy titles; Green Apple Books (✉ 506 Clement Street ☎ 415/387–2272), with new and used books, CDs and DVDs; and the Argonaut Book Shop (✉ 786 Sutter Street ☎ 415/474–9067), strong on San Francisco history, with prices to match the rarity value of many items.

XANADU GALLERY

www.xanadugallery.us/index.html

Browse Xanadu Gallery for decorative items created from amber gathered in northern California and handicrafts and jewelry from Africa and Asia.

🔒 Q5 ✉ 140 Maiden Lane ☎ 415/392–9999 🕐 Tue–Sat 10–6 🚌 2, 3, 41, 30, 45

ZONAL

www.zonalhome.com

Antique furniture, contemporary furnishings and other attention-grabbing collectibles make this store perfect for browsing.

🔒 M6 ✉ 568 Hayes Street ☎ 415/255–9307 🕐 Tue–Sat 11–6, Sun 12–5 🚌 21

A store in Chinatown

Entertainment

Once you've done with sightseeing for the day, you'll find lots of other great things to do with your time in this chapter, even if all you want to do is relax with a drink. In this section establishments are listed alphabetically.

ENTERTAINMENT

Introduction

Late-opening stores, restaurants, bars and spectacular views all enliven San Francisco after dark. Prime evening areas include North Beach, the Mission District and the Marina. The Union Square area is the hub for theater, SoMa has the latest nightclubs, while evening activities at Fisherman's Wharf are geared toward tourists, and often families.

Drinks with a View

San Francisco's topography lends itself to stunning views, and many hotels, in particular, take advantage of that. You can relax with a cocktail as you take in the view from Harry Denton's Starlight Room on the 21st-floor of the Sir Francis Drake Hotel (450 Powell Street); on weekends, the Fred Ross Project performs everything from jazz to Motown. Alternatively, have a drink in swanky Nob Hill at the Top of the Mark, a lounge on the 19th floor of the InterContinental Mark Hopkins (999 California Street) with sweeping views of the city. It offers a menu of 100 martinis, food service all day, plus afternoon tea. Or try the Marriott Hotel's 39th-floor lounge, The View (55 Fourth Street), from which it's an easy walk to SoMa or Union Square for dinner.

High-end Cocktails

Though the wine bar craze continues in San Francisco, another trend is the prevalence of the high-end cocktail: top shelf ingredients, innovative combinations and expert preparation. Many bartenders, now sometimes called

---

UP, UP AND AWAY

For a truly spectacular city adventure, take an urban helicopter flight. San Francisco Helicopter Tours (☎ 800/400–2404) offers a package that includes a flight, followed by dinner and dancing aboard the *Hornblower* yacht as it sails around the Bay.

Clockwise from top: Grant Avenue, in Chinatown, lit up at night; clubs abound in San Francisco; start the evening with a top-notch cocktail; neon lights illuminate

"mixologists," have elevated the cocktail to an art form. The upside can be a fantastic and unusual drink—or a new spin on a classic. The downside can be a longer wait at the bar. If you fancy a delicious cocktail, stop by Rickhouse (246 Kearny Street), have drinks and dinner at Beretta (▷ 142) or Bar Agricole (355 11th Street), or make a reservation at Bourbon & Branch (▷ 133), a former Prohibition-era speakeasy.

Laughs, Games and More

In addition to the city's varied bars and clubs, there are also several places to go for a laugh. Cobb's (▷ 134) and Punch Line (▷ 136) draw nationally known comedians, while BATS Improv (▷ 133) is a terrific destination for comedy on the fly. Family fun includes the Presidio Bowl (at the corner of Moraga and Montgomery), a 12-lane bowling alley in the lovely Presidio, and the arcade at the Metreon (▷ 136). The city also has movie theaters showing independent and mainstream fare.

Logistics

Most clubs and bars open nightly, from around 9pm, but are busiest around midnight, closing at 2am (some clubs stay open later, though they can't serve alcohol). Last call for many bars is about 30 minutes before closing time. While clubs in New York and Los Angeles often have a line outside to get in, that typically happens only at the hottest new spots in San Francisco. Music venues generally open 45 minutes to an hour before show time.

ENTERTAINMENT

BREWERY TOUR

To learn more about the drinks you consume in the evening, spend a few daylight hours at Anchor Brewing Company. The Potrero Hill brewery offers two free tours every weekday (reservations essential ☎ 415/863–8350; www.anchorbrewing.com), followed by a tasting session.

the street scene; the Transamerica Pyramid and the Sentinel Building at dusk

Directory

Pacific Heights to Telegraph Hill

Bars and Cafés
Buena Vista Café
Ottimista Enoteca Café
Tosca Café
Clubs/Music
Bimbo's 365 Club
Lou's Pier 47
Comedy
BATS Improv
Cobb's
Movie Theaters
Clay Theatre
Theaters
Club Fugazi
Magic Theatre

Downtown to Nob Hill

Arts Centers
Yerba Buena Center for the Arts
Bars and Cafés
Bourbon & Branch
District
House of Shields
Tonga Room
Clubs/Music
The Endup
Comedy
Punch Line
Movie Theaters
Metreon
Theaters
American Conservatory Theater
Curran Theatre

Western Addition to the Mission

Bars and Cafés
Medjool
Orbit Room
Clubs/Music
Boom Boom Room
Café du Nord
Elbo Room
The Fillmore
Great American Music Hall
The Independent
Rasselas
Slim's
Concert Halls
Louise M. Davies Symphony Hall
War Memorial Opera House
Movie Theaters
Sundance Kabuki Cinema
Theaters
Herbst Theatre
Theater Rhinoceros

Golden Gate Park

Bars and Cafés
Alembic
Toronado

Further Afield

Bars and Cafés
Café Flore
Movie Theaters
Castro Theatre

Entertainment A–Z

ALEMBIC

www.alembicbar.com
Enjoy unusual cocktails, fine beers and first-rate small plates at this chic hangout in Upper Haight.
➕ J7 ✉ 1725 Haight Street ☎ 415/666-0822 🕐 Daily noon–2am
🚌 71, N–Judah

AMERICAN CONSERVATORY THEATER

www.act-sf.org
The highly professional and thought-provoking productions here are well regarded.
➕ P5 ✉ 415 Geary Street ☎ 415/749–2228 🚌 38

BATS IMPROV

www.improv.org

Innovative improvised theater in Fort Mason (▷ 68) has been making audiences laugh for more than 25 years.

🔲 L2 ✉ B350 Fort Mason Center, Marina Boulevard at Laguna Street ☎ 415/474–6776 🚌 22, 28, 30, 49

BIMBO'S 365 CLUB

www.bimbos365club.com

Drawing crowds since 1931, this spacious North Beach club entertains with swingers, crooners and the occasional rocker.

🔲 P2 ✉ 1025 Columbus Avenue ☎ 415/474–0365 🕐 Hours vary 🚌 30; Powell–Hyde cable car

BOOM BOOM ROOM

www.boomboomblues.com

No-frills funk, jazz and blues are performed by local and national artists at this Fillmore Street venue. It was founded by the legendary blues guitarist John Lee Hooker.

🔲 L5 ✉ 1601 Fillmore Street ☎ 415/673-8000 🕐 Tue–Sun 4pm–2am 🚌 22, 38

BOURBON & BRANCH

www.bourbonandbranch.com

First-rate spirits and deft bartending are the focus at this former 1920s speakeasy in the Tenderloin (near downtown). Go online to make a reservation and get the password necessary for entry.

🔲 P5 ✉ 501 Jones Street ☎ 415/346-1735 🕐 Mon–Sat 6pm–2am 🚌 38

BUENA VISTA CAFÉ

www.thebuenavista.com

This place serves good, inexpensive food in a pricey area. It's known for its punch-packing Irish coffee.

INSIDE CAFÉS

San Francisco is renowned for its proliferation of loosely European-style cafés, found in every neighborhood, and there is no better place to check the pulse of the city. In North Beach, the legendary haunts include Caffe Greco (✉ 423 Columbus ☎ 415/397–6261), Caffe Roma (✉ 526 Columbus ☎ 415/296–7942), Caffe Trieste (✉ 609 Vallejo Street ☎ 415/982–2605) and Vesuvio (✉ 255 Columbus ☎ 415/362–3370), the stomping ground of the original Beats.

🔲 N2 ✉ 2765 Hyde Street ☎ 415/474–5044 🕐 Mon–Fri 9am–2am, Sat–Sun 8am–2am 🚌 30; Powell–Hyde cable car

CAFÉ FLORE

http://cafeflore.com

The affectionate nicknames applied to this energetic spot—such as Café Haircut and Café Bore—reflect its popularity among a mostly gay clientele.

🔲 L9 ✉ 2298 Market Street ☎ 415/621-8579 🕐 Sun–Wed 7am–12.30am, Thu–Sat 7am–2am 🚌 37, F, J, K, L, M, N

CAFÉ DU NORD

www.cafedunord.com

Hipster San Franciscans quaff cocktails in this basement bar as they listen to blues, jazz and salsa performers.

🔲 L8 ✉ 2170 Market Street ☎ 415/861-5016 🚌 37, F

CASTRO THEATRE

www.castrotheatre.com

A 1920s movie palace, complete with Wurlitzer organ, this is an atmospheric setting for cult, foreign and revival movies.

🔲 L9 ✉ 429 Castro Street ☎ 415/621-6120 🚌 24, K, L, M

CLAY THEATRE
www.landmarktheatres.com
The city's oldest continuously running cinema, built in 1910, is a favorite with San Franciscan movie buffs as the main showcase for first-run foreign movies.
➕ L4 ✉ 2261 Fillmore Street
☎ 415/267–4893 🚌 3, 22

CLUB FUGAZI
www.beachblanketbabylon.com
A zany revue, Beach Blanket Babylon, has been running for more than 35 years at this North Beach venue.
➕ P3 ✉ 678 Green Street ☎ 415/421–4222 🚌 30, 41, 45

COBB'S
www.cobbscomedyclub.com
Nationally known names top the bill at this comedy club. Reserve in advance for leading draws.
➕ P2 ✉ 915 Columbus Avenue ☎ 415/928–4320 🕐 Varies 🚌 30, 41

CURRAN THEATRE
http://shnsf.com/theatres/curran
This is one of several mainstream theaters on Geary Street and is a good choice if you want to see a Broadway blockbuster.
➕ P5 ✉ 445 Geary Street ☎ 415/551–2075 🚌 38

TICKETS
The major ticket agency, Ticketmaster, has numerous outlets at various locations including the TIX booth on Union Square. For a credit card booking or recorded information call ☎ 800/745–3000. TIX offers half-price day-of-performance tickets for Bay Area arts events from a marked booth on the southwest side of Union Square (☎ 415/433–7827).

DISTRICT
www.districtsf.com
In a sleek warehouse-style space, this wine bar has couches, a U-shape bar, dozens of wines by the glass and a lounge menu.
➕ R6 ✉ 216 Townsend Street
☎ 415/896–2120 🕐 Mon–Fri 4pm–close, Sat 5pm–close 🚌 10, 12, 30, 45

ELBO ROOM
www.elbo.com
Shoot pool downstairs, or pay a small cover for live music upstairs; acts range from Latin salsa to hip-hop to roots.
➕ M9 ✉ 647 Valencia Street
☎ 415/552–7788 🚇 16th Street–Mission
🕐 Daily 5pm–2am 🚌 14, 49

THE ENDUP
www.theendup.com
This is the biggest and most dependable of a number of gay- and lesbian-oriented nightspots, with riotous dance music.
➕ Q6 ✉ 401 6th Street ☎ 415/646–0999 🕐 Mon, Thu 10pm–4am, Fri 11pm–11am, Sat 10pm–Mon 4am; also 1st Wed of the month 5pm–4am 🚌 12, 27

THE FILLMORE
www.thefillmore.com
The legendary venue of the psych-edelic era has been revamped and now showcases Bay Area and internationally known rock bands.
➕ L5 ✉ 1805 Geary Boulevard ☎ 415/346–6000 🚌 22, 38

GREAT AMERICAN MUSIC HALL
www.musichallsf.com
See eclectic performers in a lavish setting replete with two bars, a balcony and marble columns.
➕ N5 ✉ 859 O'Farrell Street ☎ 415/885–0750 🚌 19, 38

HERBST THEATRE

www.sfwmpac.org/herbst/ht_index.html
This venue hosts chamber music, recitals and the City Arts and Lectures series.

➕ N6 ✉ War Veterans' Building, 401 Van Ness Avenue ☎ 415/392-4400 Ⓜ Civic Center or Van Ness 🚌 5, 21, 47, 49, 80X

HOUSE OF SHIELDS

www.thehouseofshields.com
One of SF's oldest bars, this unpretentious pub is popular with the post-work crowd. Recently restored, it now serves small bites to eat.

➕ Q5 ✉ 39 New Montgomery Street ☎ 415/284-9958 🕐 Mon–Fri 2pm–2am, Sat–Sun 3pm–2am Ⓜ Montgomery 🚌 14, 30, 45

THE INDEPENDENT

www.theindependentsf.com
This is a comfortable, mid-size venue for mainstream rock, jazz and hip-hop talent.

➕ K6 ✉ 628 Divisadero Street ☎ 415/771-1421 🚌 21, 24

LOUISE M. DAVIES SYMPHONY HALL

www.sfwmpac.org/symphonyhall/sh_index.html
This venue is home to the San Francisco Symphony orchestra, whose season runs September to June. Summer appearances include a pops series.

➕ N6 ✉ 201 Van Ness Avenue ☎ 415/864-6000 Ⓜ Van Ness or Civic Center 🚌 5, 21, 47, 49, 80X

LOU'S PIER 47

www.louspier47.com
The top-notch blues performers who regularly appear here draw appreciative audiences.

➕ N2 ✉ 300 Jefferson Street ☎ 415/771-5687 🕐 Mon–Fri 4pm–1am, Sat–Sun noon–1am; restaurant daily 11am–11pm 🚌 30; Powell–Hyde cable car

MAGIC THEATRE

www.magictheatre.org
This small theater has an excellent reputation; productions here range from children's plays through to political satire.

➕ M2 ✉ Building D, Fort Mason Center ☎ 415/441-8822; information 415/441-8001 🚌 22, 28, 30, 47, 49

MEDJOOL

www.medjoolsf.com
On warm evenings, crowds gather at this rooftop bar in the Mission, which offers fabulous views of San Francisco's skyline. Downstairs is a sprawling lounge and restaurant serving a selection of Mediterranean small plates.

➕ Off map ✉ 2522 Mission Street ☎ 415/550-9055 🕐 Sun–Thu 4pm–11pm, Fri–Sat 4pm–1.30am Ⓜ 24th Street–Mission 🚌 14

METREON
www.westfield.com/metreon
This five-story behemoth has movie theaters, a giant IMAX screen, an arcade with interactive games and various dining options.
✚ Q5 ✉ 101 4th Street ☎ 415/369-6000 🚌 14, 30, 45, 71

ORBIT ROOM
Floor-to-ceiling windows overlook Market Street at this lounge, with a circular bar, which serves innovative drinks made with painstaking care.
✚ M7 ✉ 1900 Market Street ☎ 415/252-9525 🕐 Mon–Fri 5pm–close, Sat–Sun noon–close 🚌 Any Market Street bus

OTTIMISTA ENOTECA CAFÉ
www.ottimistasf.com
Ottimista has a rotating list of 35–40 wines by the glass and a small seasonal menu.
✚ M3 ✉ 1838 Union Street ☎ 415/674-8400 🕐 Tue–Thu 2pm–11pm, Fri noon–2am, Sat 11am–2am, Sun 11am–10pm 🚌 41, 45

PUNCH LINE
www.punchlinecomedyclub.com
This long-running venue for both aspiring and nationally known comedians has a good record of giving future stars their early break.
✚ Q4 ✉ 444 Battery Street ☎ 415/397-7573 🚌 3, 41

RASSELAS
www.rasselasjazzclub.com
At this combined jazz and supper club you can savor Ethiopian food and listen to some of the better local combos.
✚ L5 ✉ 1534 Fillmore Street 415/346-8696 🕐 Daily 5pm–1.30am 🚌 22, 38

SLIM'S
www.slims-sf.com
The excellent sound system and convivial atmosphere make this one of San Francisco's best club-size music spots for quality rock, jazz or rhythm and blues acts most nights.
✚ P7 ✉ 333 11th Street ☎ 415/255-0333 🚌 9, 12

SUNDANCE KABUKI CINEMA
www.sundancecinemas.com
This eight-screen modern movie complex is in Japantown.
✚ L5 ✉ 1881 Post Street, at Fillmore Street ☎ 415/929-4650 🚌 2, 3, 38

THEATER RHINOCEROS
www.therhino.org
The diverse offerings at the home of the US's first gay and lesbian theater company often explore social attitudes and behavior. The theater was founded in 1977.
✚ N8 ✉ 1360 Mission Street, Suite #200 ☎ 800/838-3006 🚌 14

TONGA ROOM
www.tongaroom.com
This Nob Hill bar is full of kitsch, rum drinks and even periodic tropical rainstorms.

P4 ✉ Fairmont Hotel, 950 Mason Street
☎ 415/772–5278 ◷ Wed–Sun 5pm–1am
🚋 1; Powell–Hyde cable car

TORONADO
www.toronado.com
The various alternative lifestyles
that are part and parcel of the
Haight-Ashbury neighborhood can
be observed at this lively haunt.
L7 ✉ 547 Haight Street ☎ 415/863–
2276 ◷ Daily 11.30am–2am 🚌 6, 66, 71

TOSCA CAFÉ
www.toscacafesf.com
Opened in 1919 and allegedly
serving the first espresso in

Chinatown at night

California, Tosca has opera
reverberating from its jukebox
and numerous celebrity regulars
including Nicolas Cage and Francis
Ford Coppola.
Q3 ✉ 242 Columbus Avenue
☎ 415/986–9651 ◷ Tue, Sun 5pm–
midnight, Wed–Sat 5pm–2am 🚌 41

WAR MEMORIAL OPERA HOUSE
www.sfwmpac.org/operahouse/oh_index.
html
From September to December,
this is the venue for the San
Francisco Opera season. From
February to May, the San Francisco
Ballet appears here and it returns
at Christmas for the Nutcracker.
N6 ✉ 301 Van Ness Avenue
☎ 415/621–6600 🚇 Van Ness or Civic
Center 🚌 5, 21, 47, 49, 80

YERBA BUENA CENTER FOR THE ARTS
www.ybca.org
This state-of-the art venue (▷ 63),
with a 775-seat theater, has a
strong program of contemporary
music, dance and drama.
Q5 ✉ 701 Mission Street
☎ 415/978–2787 🚇 Powell Street
🚌 14, 30, 45

ENTERTAINMENT

PLAT DU JOUR

• SPECIALS •

Soups

- FRENCH ONION
- VEGETABLE w/ ORzo

Special

BLT with goat cheese
on our homemade,
organic ciabatta.

Come in for a glass
of beer or wine and
a salad or sandwich!

Eat

There are places to eat across the city to suit all tastes and budgets. In this section establishments are listed alphabetically.

Introduction

If Los Angeles has the lock on celebrities, then San Francisco has the lock on celebrity chefs—and first-rate chefs of the non-celebrity variety as well. When leading food magazines like *Bon Appetit* and *Gourmet* rank America's dining cities, San Francisco always rises to the top of the list, and for very good reason.

Culinary Melting Pot

With thousands of restaurants to choose from, it's difficult to think of a cuisine that can't be found here: *dim sum* that can compete with any you would find in Hong Kong; inexpensive, delicious and filling burritos, particularly good in the Mission District; increasingly good options for Indian and Pakistani food; unbelievably fresh sushi; enticing French bakeries; California cuisine in its many incarnations; plus great food influenced by Latin America, Asia and Europe.

Alice Waters

Of course, the culinary wonders aren't limited to San Francisco. Across the Bay is Berkeley's doyenne of food, Alice Waters. Her restaurant, Chez Panisse (▷ 112), is 40 years old, but her famously simple fare isn't showing signs of age. She "pioneered" a concept that has actually been around since the beginning of time: using seasonal, organic, local ingredients. She has influenced chefs domestically and abroad with her unpretentious menus that allow the fresh ingredients to assume the starring role.

EAT LIKE A SAN FRANCISCAN

Along with sustainable agriculture and socially responsible eating, the other trend that shows no sign of slowing down is the "small plates" craze. While some bemoan the practice, others embrace it as an opportunity to try extra dishes on the menu. Chefs are typically more inventive with appetizers and small plates, so be adventurous and sample a few.

From top: A tempting steak; a café in Haight-Ashbury; preparing shellfish at a restaurant in the Fisherman's Wharf area; a restaurant kitchen on Market Street

EAT

Directory

The Presidio

American
Liverpool Lil's
Presidio Social Club
Asian
Kabuto
Khan Toke
Ton Kiang
French
Baker Street Bistro
Italian
A16
Spruce
Mexican/Latin American
Mamacita

Pacific Heights to Telegraph Hill

American
Barney's Gourmet Hamburgers
Gary Danko
Izzy's Steaks & Chops
Asian
Ana Mandara
Betelnut
French
Café des Amis
Italian
Mario's Bohemian Cigar Store
North Beach Pizza
Rose Pistola
Mexican
Tacolicious
Spanish
Zarzuela
Vegetarian
Greens

Downtown to Nob Hill

American
Americano
Bix
Boulevard
Dottie's True Blue Café
Town Hall
Wayfare Tavern

Asian
Le Colonial
House of Nanking
Lucky Creation
Shalimar
Silks
Slanted Door
French
Café Claude
Fleur de Lys
Fringale
Plouf
Greek
Kokkari Estiatorio
Italian
Perbacco

Western Addition to the Mission

American
Little Star Pizza
Max's
Monk's Kettle
Nopa
Asian
Dosa
Mifune
Tsunami Sushi & Sake Bar
Italian
Beretta
Delfina
Flour + Water
Mexican/Latin American
Charanga
Taqueria Cancun

Golden Gate Park

Asian
Indian Oven
Thep Phanom

Further Afield

Asian
Eric's Restaurant

EAT

Eating A–Z

<table>
<tr><td colspan="2">**PRICES**</td></tr>
<tr><td colspan="2">Prices are approximate, based on a 3-course meal for one person.</td></tr>
<tr><td>$$$$</td><td>over $50</td></tr>
<tr><td>$$$</td><td>$31–$50</td></tr>
<tr><td>$$</td><td>$15–$30</td></tr>
<tr><td>$</td><td>under $15</td></tr>
</table>

A16 $$$

www.a16sf.com

You'll find wood-fired pizzas, dishes from Italy's Campania region and a wine list focusing on Southern Italian and California wines here.

🞧 K3 ✉ 2355 Chestnut Street ☎ 415/771–2216 ⏱ Wed–Fri lunch and dinner, Sat–Tue dinner 🚌 24, 30

AMERICANO $$$

www.americanorestaurant.com

In the Hotel Vitale, this restaurant serves tasty California cuisine. The spacious outdoor patio becomes a singles magnet after work.

🞧 R4 ✉ 8 Mission Street ☎ 415/278–3777 ⏱ Breakfast daily; Mon–Fri lunch and dinner, Sat dinner 🚌 1, 14, 49

Pizza is a popular option

ANA MANDARA $$$

www.anamandara.com

Who would have thought that Vietnamese food in such elegant surroundings could exist in Ghirardelli Square? The upstairs bar is a perfect pre- or post-dinner spot.

🞧 N2 ✉ 891 Beach Street ☎ 415/771–6800 ⏱ Mon–Fri lunch and dinner, Sat–Sun dinner 🚌 19, 30; Powell–Hyde cable car

BAKER STREET BISTRO $$–$$$

www.bakerstreetbistro.com

Patrons tolerate cramped quarters in return for fantastic bistro fare at stunningly good prices.

🞧 K3 ✉ 2953 Baker Street ☎ 415/931–1475 ⏱ Tue–Fri lunch and dinner, Sat–Sun brunch and dinner 🚌 41, 45, 76

BARNEY'S GOURMET HAMBURGERS $–$$

www.barneyshamburgers.com

Enjoy fantastic burgers, curly fries and shakes, plus healthier options like soups and salads. The outdoor patio is an added bonus. There's another branch in Noe Valley (4138 24th Street), plus four East Bay locations.

🞧 L3 ✉ 3344 Steiner Street ☎ 415/563–0307 ⏱ Daily lunch and dinner 🚌 24, 30

BERETTA $$

www.berettasf.com

This Italian restaurant in the Mission District focuses on delicious thin-crust pizzas and cocktails crafted with expertise. For groups smaller than six, call ahead to add your name to the waiting list.

🞧 Off map ✉ 1199 Valencia Street ☎ 415/695–1199 ⏱ Mon–Fri dinner, Sat–Sun brunch, lunch and dinner 🚇 24th Street–Mission 🚌 14, 49

BETELNUT $$$

www.betelnutrestaurant.com

Asian fusion cuisine and great cocktails are the draw at this consistent Pacific Heights spot.

🏠 L3 ✉ 2030 Union Street ☎ 415/929–8855 🕐 Daily lunch and dinner 🚌 41, 45

BIX $$$$

www.bixrestaurant.com

Tucked away on a downtown alley, this atmospheric supper club is always packed.

🏠 Q3 ✉ 56 Gold Street (between Jackson and Pacific streets) ☎ 415/433–6300 🕐 Daily dinner 🚌 3, 41

BOULEVARD $$$$

www.boulevardrestaurant.com

Try to nab a seat in the back room of this Embarcadero restaurant where you can gaze at Bay Bridge as you dive into superb New American cuisine. Dishes may include Sonoma foie gras, roasted sea bass and filet mignon.

🏠 R4 ✉ 1 Mission Street ☎ 415/543–6084 🕐 Mon–Fri lunch and dinner, Sat–Sun dinner 🚌 1, 14, 41

CAFÉ DES AMIS $$$

www.cafedesamissf.com

A French newcomer in Cow Hollow, this brasserie has sleek black wood and marble floors. Menu items run the gamut from steak frites to lamb's tongue salad. There's a lively bar scene.

🏠 L3 ✉ 2000 Union Street ☎ 415/563–7700 🕐 Daily lunch and dinner 🚌 41, 45

CAFÉ CLAUDE $$

www.cafeclaude.com

Quintessentially French dishes like salad nicoise and onion soup are served in the downtown French quarter of the city, by Gallic waiters with a bit of attitude.

🏠 Q4 ✉ 7 Claude Lane (between Grant and Kearny streets) 🕐 Mon–Sat lunch and dinner, Sun dinner ☎ 415/392–3515 🚌 2, 3, 45

CHARANGA $$

www.charangasf.com

Charanga is a bustling Mission District eatery with a loyal following for its Caribbean and Latin American-style tapas.

🏠 N9 ✉ 2351 Mission Street ☎ 415/282–1813 🕐 Tue–Fri dinner, Sat–Sun brunch and dinner 🚇 16th Street–Mission 🚌 14, 49

LE COLONIAL $$$

www.lecolonialsf.com

The ambience here evokes French-colonial Vietnam and a veranda beckons for fine-weather dining. Sample a snack from the bar or sit down to fully experience the California reworkings of Vietnamese dishes.

🏠 P5 ✉ 20 Cosmo Place ☎ 415/931–3600 🕐 Mon–Fri dinner, Sat–Sun brunch, dinner 🚌 1, 2, 3, 27, 31, 76

EAT

SOURDOUGH BREAD

The slightly bitter and chewy sourdough bread served in many San Franciscan restaurants first appeared here during the Gold Rush (and was first baked commercially by a French San Franciscan settler named Isadore Boudin). Yeast and baking powder were scarce and settlers made bread using a sour starter, a fermented mixture of flour and water that enabled the dough to rise. San Franciscan folklore holds that the quality of a sourdough loaf is dependent upon environmental conditions—in particular, the local fog.

DELFINA $$$

www.delfinasf.com

This Mission District trattoria serves its customers simple, delicious dishes that are made from top-notch ingredients.

➕ M9 ✉ 3621 18th Street ☎ 415/552–4055 🕐 Daily dinner 🚇 16th Street–Mission 🚌 14, 33

DOSA $$–$$$

www.dosasf.com

Enjoy South Indian fare in elegant surroundings in the Fillmore District. The original, smaller restaurant is in the Mission District (995 Valencia Street).

➕ L5 ✉ 1700 Fillmore Street ☎ 415/441–3672 🕐 Mon–Tue dinner, Wed–Sun lunch and dinner 🚌 22, 38

DOTTIE'S TRUE BLUE CAFÉ $$

This small, friendly diner close to Union Square serves up great start-the-day omelets. Later in the day, you can choose from a variety of healthy lunches.

➕ P5 ✉ 522 Jones Street ☎ 415/885–2767 🕐 Wed–Mon breakfast and lunch 🚌 27

ERIC'S RESTAURANT $$

Delicious Hunan and Mandarin cuisine is served in a clean white dining room overflowing with Noe Valley locals.

➕ Off map M9 ✉ 1500 Church Street ☎ 415/282–0919 🕐 Daily lunch and dinner 🚌 24, J

FLEUR DE LYS $$$$

www.fleurdelyssf.com

Fleur de Lys is more formal than many restaurants—jacket and tie are required—and serves San Francisco's best French food.

➕ P5 ✉ 777 Sutter Street ☎ 415/673–7779 🕐 Tue–Sat dinner 🚌 2, 3

FLOUR + WATER $$$

www.flourandwater.com

The small menu of seasonal Italian fare at this lauded restaurant typically includes home-made pastas, Neopolitan-style pizzas and cured meats. The oven was imported from Italy.

➕ P9 ✉ 2401 Harrison Street ☎ 415/826–7000 🕐 Daily dinner 🚌 12, 27

FRINGALE $$$

www.fringalesf.com

Basque-French cuisine is dished up in an intimate but casual bistro close to the Metreon. The dessert menu is extensive and irresistible.

➕ R6 ✉ 570 4th Street ☎ 415/543–0573 🕐 Tue–Fri lunch and dinner, Sat–Mon dinner 🚇 Powell Street or Montgomery Street 🚌 9, 30, 45

GARY DANKO $$$$

www.garydanko.com

This is one of the city's finest restaurants, located in Russian Hill; choose from the three- to five-course tasting menu. The service is impeccable.

➕ N2 ✉ 800 North Point Street ☎ 415/749–2060 🕐 Daily dinner 🚌 19, 30; Powell–Hyde cable car

GREENS $$$

www.greensrestaurant.com

Greens offers gourmet-pleasing vegetarian dishes using the produce of an organic farm run at

For a taste of Japan, try sushi

a Zen Buddhist retreat on the north side of San Francisco Bay. The bay views are as stunning as the food. Reserve ahead.
➕ M2 ✉ Building A, Fort Mason Center ☎ 415/771–6222 ⏰ Tue–Sat lunch and dinner, Sun brunch and dinner 🚌 22, 28, 30, 47, 49

HOUSE OF NANKING $
This tiny, popular eatery in Chinatown was among the first to bring Shanghai and northern Chinese cooking to San Francisco.
➕ Q3 ✉ 919 Kearny Street ☎ 415/421–1429 ⏰ Daily lunch and dinner 🚌 30, 41

INDIAN OVEN $$
www.indianovensf.com
This Haight spot whips up some of the best tandoori, naan and curry dishes in town.
➕ L7 ✉ 233 Fillmore Street ☎ 415/626–1628 ⏰ Daily lunch and dinner 🚌 6, 22, 66, 71

IZZY'S STEAKS & CHOPS $$$
www.izzyssteaks.com
A carnivore's paradise in the Marina, Izzy's Steaks and Chops focuses on tender steak in all cuts and sizes.
➕ L3 ✉ 3345 Steiner Street ☎ 415/563–0487 ⏰ Mon–Sat dinner, Sun brunch and dinner 🚌 22, 76

KABUTO $$–$$$
www.kabutosushi.com
A no-frills atmosphere at this Richmond District sushi bar keeps the focus on fresh raw fish.
➕ F6 ✉ 5121 Geary Boulevard ☎ 415/752–5652 ⏰ Tue–Sat lunch and dinner, Sun dinner 🚌 2, 29, 38

> ### DIM SUM
> Popular at lunchtime and for weekend brunch, dim sum consists of various small dishes offered to diners from carts. The cost is determined by the number of empty dishes on your table. Favorite dim sum dishes include *cha sil bow*—steamed pork bun; *chern goon*—spring rolls; *gai bow*—steamed chicken bun; and *sil mi*—steamed pork and shrimp dumplings. Rather less popular among Westerners are *gai guerk*—braised chicken feet; and *op guerk*—braised duck's feet.

KHAN TOKE $$

In this Richmond restaurant guests remove their shoes before dining on top-notch Thai cuisine at sunken tables.

🔢 E6 ✉ 5937 Geary Boulevard
☎ 415/668–6654 🕐 Daily dinner
🚌 2, 29, 38

KOKKARI ESTIATORIO $$$

www.kokkari.com

This Financial District taverna serves classic Greek favorites including *spanakopita* (spinach pie), moussaka and lamb dishes.

🔢 R3 ✉ 200 Jackson Street ☎ 415/981–0983 🕐 Mon–Fri lunch and dinner, Sat–Sun dinner 🚇 Embarcadero 🚌 3, 12

LITTLE STAR PIZZA $$

www.littlestarpizza.com

Listen to the jukebox while you wait for tantalizing Chicago-style pizza in the Western Addition. (You'll find another branch in the Mission District.)

🔢 K6 ✉ 846 Divisadero Street ☎ 415/441–1118 🕐 Tue–Sun dinner 🚌 24

LIVERPOOL LIL'S $$$

www.liverpoollils.com

It's a crime not to get a beer with your meal at this Pacific Heights saloon-cum-burger joint. You can dine on the sidewalk when weather permits.

🔢 J3 ✉ 2942 Lyon Street ☎ 415/921–6664 🕐 Mon–Fri lunch and dinner, Sat–Sun brunch, lunch and dinner
🚌 30, 41, 45

LUCKY CREATION $

This tiny Chinatown hideaway serves adventurous vegetarian, and a few vegan, versions of Chinese food, including dim sum.

🔢 Q4 ✉ 854 Washington Street 🕐 Thu–Tue lunch and dinner ☎ 415/989–0818
🚌 30, 45

MAMACITA $$

www.mamacitasf.com

The upscale authentic Mexican fare at this cantina comes with a lively singles scene at the bar and quite a bit of noise.

🔢 K3 ✉ 2317 Chestnut Street
☎ 415/346–8494 🕐 Daily dinner
🚌 24, 30

MARIO'S BOHEMIAN CIGAR STORE $

This long-established North Beach café offers some excellent focaccia bread snacks.

🔢 P3 ✉ 566 Columbus Avenue
☎ 415/362–0536 🕐 Daily lunch and dinner 🚌 30, 41, 45

MAX'S $–$$

www.maxsworld.com

While the New York-style deli fare is affordable and filling at this Bay Area chain, the real attraction for many customers is the opera-singing staff.

🔢 N6 ✉ 601 Van Ness Avenue
☎ 415/771–7301 🕐 Mon–Fri lunch and dinner, Sat–Sun brunch, lunch and dinner
🚌 5, 47, 49

VEGETARIANS

If you don't eat meat, you still have plenty of dining options in the City by the Bay. In addition to Greens (▷ 144), noteworthy vegetarian establishments include Ananda Fuara (✉ 1298 Market Street ☎ 415/621–1994), in the Civic Center, and Millennium (✉ 580 Geary Street ☎ 415/345–3900), which serves imaginative organic and dairy-free entrées. Most Chinese and Indian restaurants also offer numerous vegetarian dishes.

Bread and cheese make a tasty snack...

...or try some seafood

MIFUNE $

www.mifune.com

Fast-food Japanese-style is served to fast-moving customers here; the noodle dishes are excellent.

🖪 L5 ✉ Japan Center, 1737 Post Street, Japantown ☎ 415/922-0337 ⏰ Daily lunch and dinner 🚌 38

MONK'S KETTLE $$

www.monkskettle.com

This Mission District gastropub serves small and large plates meant to pair nicely with the dozens of beers on the menu. It stays open until late.

🖪 M8 ✉ 3141 16th Street ☎ 415/865-9523 ⏰ Daily lunch and dinner 🚇 16th Street–Mission 🚌 22, 26

NOPA $$$

www.nopasf.com

Short for "north of the Panhandle", this former bank in the Western Addition now serves organic California fare past midnight in a lively, loud atmosphere.

🖪 K7 ✉ 560 Divisadero Street ☎ 415/864-8643 ⏰ Mon–Fri dinner, Sat–Sun brunch and dinner 🚌 24

NORTH BEACH PIZZA $

www.northbeachpizza.com

The thick, chewy pizzas with a host of toppings, famous throughout the city, often result in a line outside in the evening; other locations include 800 Stanyan Street.

🖪 Q3 ✉ 1462 Grant Avenue ☎ 415/433-2444 ⏰ Daily lunch and dinner 🚌 30, 41, 45

PERBACCO $$$

www.perbaccosf.com

This downtown Italian gets high marks for its Piedmont and Ligurian cuisine.

🖪 R4 ✉ 230 California Street ☎ 415/955-0663 ⏰ Mon–Fri lunch and dinner, Sat dinner 🚌 1, 41; California Street cable car

PLOUF $$–$$$

www.ploufsf.com

You can eat outdoors at this downtown bistro on a pedestrian-only alley. Tasty seafood is the focus; mussels are the house specialty.

🖪 Q4 ✉ 40 Belden Place ☎ 415/986-6491 ⏰ Mon–Fri lunch and dinner, Sat dinner 🚌 1, 3, 30, 45, 76

PRESIDIO SOCIAL CLUB $$$

www.presidiosocialclub.com

Once an old army barracks, this Presidio restaurant now serves classic cocktails and American comfort food, like roast chicken and macaroni and cheese.

✚ J3 ✉ 563 Ruger Street ☎ 415/885–1888 ⏱ Daily lunch and dinner; also brunch Sat–Sun 🚌 28, 29, 41, 43, 45

ROSE PISTOLA $$$

www.rosepistolasf.com

This North Beach haunt has an open kitchen, wood-burning oven and a menu inspired by the cuisine of Italy's Liguria region. There's live jazz Friday to Sunday.

✚ P3 ✉ 532 Columbus Avenue ☎ 415/399–0499 ⏱ Daily lunch and dinner 🚌 30, 41, 45

SHALIMAR $

www.shalimarsf.com

Great naan is the tip of the iceberg at this budget Indian-Pakistani spot in the dodgy Tenderloin. There's a second branch on Polk. Cash only.

✚ P5 ✉ 532 Jones Street ☎ 415/928–0333 ⏱ Daily lunch and dinner 🚌 38

SILKS $$$$

www.mandarinoriental.com/sanfrancisco/dining/silks

A blend of contemporary American cuisine and Asian subtlety is found at the restaurant of the Mandarin Oriental hotel.

✚ Q4 ✉ Mandarin Oriental, 222 Sansome Street ☎ 415/986–2020 ⏱ Breakfast daily; Mon lunch, Tue–Friday lunch and dinner, Sat dinner, Sun brunch 🚌 1, 2, 41; California Street cable car

SLANTED DOOR $$$

www.slanteddoor.com

Slanted Door serves modern Vietnamese cuisine in a spacious setting overlooking the Bay. For quicker, cheaper fare, visit Out the Door, the restaurant's to-go counter in the Ferry Building's main hall.

✚ R4 ✉ 1 Ferry Building ☎ 415/861–8032 ⏱ Daily lunch and dinner 🚌 2, 6, 9, 14, 21, 31

SPRUCE $$$$

www.sprucesf.com

This Laurel Heights restaurant serves a Mediterranean- and Italian-influenced menu in

Mexican tortilla chips and a bean dip

A plate of dim sum

sophisticated, inviting surroundings.

J5 ✉ 3640 Sacramento Street
☎ 415/931-5100 🕐 Mon–Fri lunch and
dinner, Sat–Sun dinner 🚌 1, 3, 43

TACOLICIOUS $–$$

www.tacolicioussf.com
Fresh, flavorful tacos and ceviche
offset the cramped, loud quarters
at this new Marina favorite.

L3 ✉ 2031 Chestnut Street
☎ 415/346-1966 🕐 Daily lunch and
dinner 🚌 22, 30

TAQUERIA CANCUN $

Burritos in many varieties and
other well-prepared Mexican
favorites are found in this busy eatery in the Mission District. Another
location is at 3211 Mission.

N9 ✉ 2288 Mission Street
☎ 415/252-9560 🕐 Daily breakfast, lunch
and dinner 🚌 14, 49

THEP PHANOM $$

www.thepphanom.com
Hot Thai cuisine is served here, in
the Lower Heights neighborhood.

L7 ✉ 400 Waller Street ☎ 415/431-
2526 🕐 Daily dinner 🚌 6, 22, 66, 71

TON KIANG $$

www.tonkiang.net
Spread over two Richmond District
floors and frequented mainly
for its excellent Hong-Kong style
dim sum, Ton Kiang also offers a
Hakka-style dinner menu.

E6 ✉ 5821 Geary Boulevard
☎ 415/387-8273 🕐 Daily lunch and
dinner 🚌 2, 29, 38

TOWN HALL $$$

www.townhallsf.com
This former warehouse turned
SoMa restaurant focuses on
regional American fare with New

Orleans influences. Menus have
included buttermilk fried chicken
and cornmeal fried oysters.

R5 ✉ 342 Howard Street ☎ 415/908-
3900 🕐 Mon–Sat lunch and dinner,
Sun dinner 🚌 6, 10, N–Judah

TSUNAMI SUSHI & SAKE BAR $$$

www.dajanigroup.net/establishments/
tsunami-sushi-panhandle
Dine on unusual rolls at low tables
at this hip Western Addition sushi
spot with countless sake options.

K6 ✉ 1306 Fulton Street ☎ 415/567-
7664 🕐 Mon–Sat dinner 🚌 24

WAYFARE TAVERN $$$

www.wayfaretavern.com
Celebrity chef Tyler Florence's
three-story Financial District restaurant serves American fare in a
men's club-style atmosphere.

Q4 ✉ 558 Sacramento Street
☎ 415/772-9060 🕐 Mon–Sat lunch and
dinner, Sun dinner 🚌 1, 3, 8X, 10, 12, 30,
41; California Street cable car

ZARZUELA $$–$$$

If you can brave the dire parking
situation in Russian Hill, the
Spanish tapas, paella and sangria
here are worth the effort.

N3 ✉ 2000 Hyde Street ☎ 415/346-
0800 🕐 Tue–Sat dinner 🚌 41, 45;
Powell–Hyde cable car

EAT

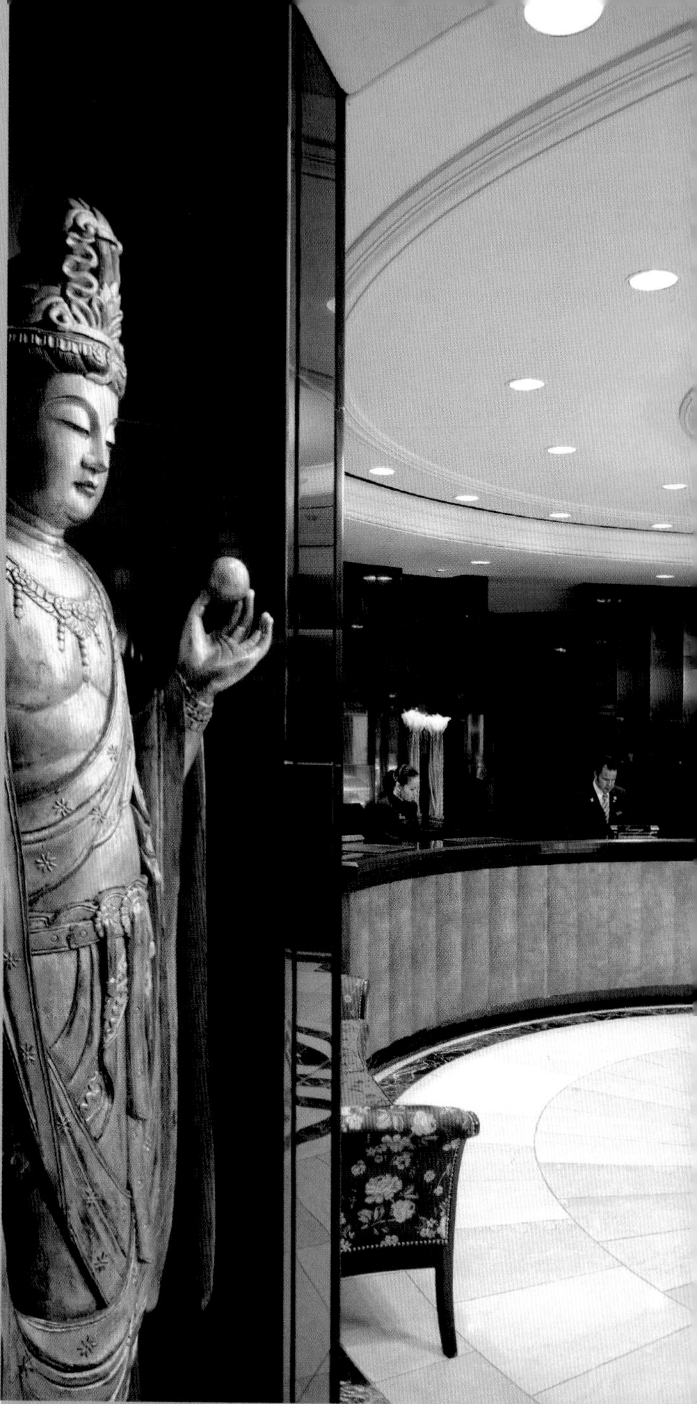

Sleep

Ranging from luxurious and modern upmarket hotels to simple budget hostels, San Francisco has accommodation to suit everyone. In this section establishments are listed alphabetically.

Introduction

San Francisco has a huge range of accommodations. The city is compact and fairly easy to navigate by public transportation or by car, so location here is less important than it is in larger cities. Booking ahead is crucial, however, especially during high season.

Hotels

Full-service hotels are primarily in the downtown, SoMa and Nob Hill neighborhoods of San Francisco. You'll pay more, of course, for the location and the amenities, which will likely include a fitness room or gym, laundry service, in-room internet access and safes, valet parking and concierge. Swimming pools are not as prevalent in San Francisco as they are in Los Angeles, but several hotels have them. Most hotels do not include breakfast or parking in their rates, but many allow children to share a room with their parents free of charge.

Motels

Many motels belong to chains and offer reliability and good value; they're ideal for a brief stopover. The majority of San Francisco's motels are along Lombard Street in the Marina District, in the northern section of the city. The street is a busy thoroughfare to the Golden Gate Bridge and Highway 101, but it's also near shops, restaurants and some notable attractions. Motels typically offer cable TV and hair dryers.

OTHER OPTIONS

There are a number of hostels in San Francisco that charge as little as $25–$30 per night per person. Most have single-sex dorms, although some may also have family rooms. Contact American Youth Hostels (www.hiusa.org). B&Bs can be a more personal alternative to a hotel, but keep in mind that they often require two-night minimum stays on weekends and three-night minimum stays during holidays.

San Francisco has a large choice of accommodations, but be sure to book ahead

SLEEP

Directory

The Presidio

Mid-Range
Laurel Inn

Pacific Heights to Telegraph Hill

Budget
Hostelling International San
   Francisco Fisherman's Wharf
San Remo Hotel
Town House Motel
Mid-Range
Best Western Tuscan Inn
Hotel Boheme
Hotel Majestic
Hotel del Sol
Marina Motel
Luxury
Argonaut Hotel
Hotel Drisco
Washington Square Inn

Downtown to Nob Hill

Budget
Adelaide Hotel & Hostel
Hostelling International San
   Francisco City Center
Hostelling International San
   Francisco Downtown
Hotel des Arts
Hotel Metropolis
Mid-Range
Hotel Bijou
Hotel Diva
Hotel Frank
Hotel Griffon
Hotel Rex
Renoir Hotel

Luxury
Campton Place
Clift Hotel
Fairmont Hotel and Tower
Four Seasons
Mandarin Oriental
The Palace Hotel
Ritz-Carlton San Francisco
Westin St. Francis
White Swan Inn
W Hotel

Western Addition to the Mission

Budget
Elements Hotel
Mid-Range
Best Western Hotel Tomo
Chateau Tivoli
Inn at the Opera
Phoenix Hotel
Sleep Over Sauce

Golden Gate Park

Mid-Range
Red Victorian Bed, Breakfast & Art
Stanyan Park Hotel

Further Afield

Budget
24 Henry
Willows Inn
Mid-Range
Village House

Sleeping A–Z

24 HENRY $

www.24henry.com

A five-room guest house in the Castro district, 24 Henry is run by and chiefly aimed at gay men. Breakfast is included.
➕ L9 ✉ 24 Henry Street ☎ 800/900–5686 or 415/864–5686 🚌 24, 37

ADELAIDE HOTEL & HOSTEL $

www.adelaidehostel.com

This Financial District pension offers dorms, private rooms and rooms for families (up to four people) at the original location and in two nearby buildings on Post.
➕ P5 ✉ 5 Isadora Duncan Court (off Taylor Street, between Geary and

BED-AND-BREAKFAST

San Francisco's bed-and-breakfast inns offer a friendly alternative to hotels. Bed-and-breakfast owners often serve a healthy home-cooked breakfast, and will readily pass on their knowledge of the city. Reflecting the fact that both the individual properties and the rooms within them can vary greatly, bed-and-breakfast establishments span all price categories and are found all over the city. Advance reservation is always recommended. Bed-and-breakfast accommodations can be arranged through Bed & Breakfast San Francisco; for reservations go online at www.bbsf.com or telephone ☎ 800/452–8249.

Post streets) ☎ 877/359–1915 or 415/359–1915 🚌 2, 3, 38, 76

ARGONAUT HOTEL $$$

www.argonauthotel.com

The nautical theme at this Fisherman's Wharf hotel is fitting for its location. Rooms are airy, WiFi is complimentary. It's pet-friendly and has 265 rooms.
➕ N2 ✉ 495 Jefferson Street ☎ 415/563–0800 or 866/415–0704 🚌 19, 30, 47, 91, F; Powell–Hyde cable car

BEST WESTERN HOTEL TOMO $$

www.jdvhotels.com/tomo

This Japantown Best Western has Japanese pop art, a wall of TVs playing movies in the lobby, and gaming suites, plus 125 rooms.
➕ L5 ✉ 1800 Sutter Street ☎ 415/921–4000 or 888/822–8666 🚌 2, 3, 76

BEST WESTERN TUSCAN INN $$

www.tuscaninn.com

Coffee and biscotti are included at this Fisherman's Wharf hotel with 221 rooms on four floors. Pets are allowed.
➕ P2 ✉ 425 North Point Street ☎ 415/561–1100 or 800/648–4626 🚌 30

CAMPTON PLACE $$$

www.tajhotels.com/camptonplace

Well placed close to Union Square, Campton Place has 110 stylish rooms and attentive staff.
➕ Q5 ✉ 340 Stockton Street ☎ 415/781–5555 🚌 30, 45

CHATEAU TIVOLI $$

www.chateautivoli.com

An amiable and historic Victorian B&B near Alamo Square, Chateau

Tivoli has nine rooms and suites. It serves a generous weekend brunch, as well as afternoon cheese and wine.

➕ L6 ✉ 1057 Steiner Street ☎ 415/776–5462 or 800/228–1647 🚌 5, 21

CLIFT HOTEL $$$

www.clifthotel.com

This Philippe Starck-designed hotel has a whimsical lobby, 378 guest rooms, and the famed art deco-style Redwood Room bar.

➕ P5 ✉ 495 Geary Street ☎ 415/775–4700 or 800/697–1791 🚌 38

ELEMENTS HOTEL $

www.elementssf.com

Elements is a chic, ultramodern Mission District hotel with hostel-like prices. Private and shared rooms are available, and the hotel sits adjacent to the hip, Mediterranean-themed Medjool restaurant and bar (▷ 136).

➕ Off map ✉ 2516 Mission Street ☎ 415/647–4100, 866/327–8407 🚇 24th Street–Mission 🚌 14

FAIRMONT HOTEL AND TOWER $$$

www.fairmont.com/sanfrancisco

This famous Nob Hill landmark hotel has 591 sumptuous tower rooms affording lovely views.

➕ P4 ✉ 950 Mason Street ☎ 800/441–1414 or 415/ 772–5000 🚌 1; Powell–Hyde cable car

FOUR SEASONS $$$

www.fourseasons.com/sanfrancisco

This elegant hotel has 277 spacious rooms and suites. Guests can use the Sports Club/LA gym.

➕ Q5 ✉ 757 Market Street ☎ 415/633–3000 or 800/819–5053 🚌 Any Market Street bus

TELEPHONING HOTELS

Many hotels and some bed-and-breakfast inns can be telephoned using toll-free numbers (prefixed 800, 888, 877 or 866). Remember that these numbers can usually be dialed from anywhere in the United States or Canada, although there is sometimes a different toll-free number for calls made within California (and a few numbers may be available in California only).

HOSTELLING INTERNATIONAL SAN FRANCISCO $

www.sfhostels.com

More than 600 hostel beds, mostly in small dorms with some private rooms, are available at the three sites of Hostelling International: City Center, Downtown and Fisherman's Wharf (Fort Mason). All three offer luggage storage, self-catering kitchens and internet access, and all can be easily reached by bus.

City Center ➕ N5 ✉ 685 Ellis Street ☎ 415/474–5721 🚌 27

Downtown ➕ P5 ✉ 312 Mason Street ☎ 415/788–5604 🚌 38

Fisherman's Wharf ➕ M2 ✉ Building 240, Fort Mason ☎ 415/771–7277 🚌 28, 49

HOTEL DES ARTS $–$$

www.sfhoteldesarts.com

As the name suggests, local artists have decorated this hotel, and their work also features in the gallery. The least costly of the 43 rooms have washbasins and shared bathrooms, while others have private facilities. A continental breakfast is served.

➕ Q4 ✉ 447 Bush Street ☎ 800/956–4322 or 415/ 956–3232 🚌 2, 3, 76

SLEEP

Reservations should be made as early as possible. A deposit (usually by credit card) equivalent to the nightly rate should ensure your room is held at least until 6pm; if you are arriving later, inform the hotel. Credit card is the usual payment method; traveler's checks or cash can be used but payment will then be expected in advance. The total charge will include the city's 14 percent accommodations tax.

HOTEL BIJOU $$

www.hotelbijou.com
San Francisco-set movies provide the cue for the 65 theme rooms here, close to Union Square. Breakfast is included.
➕ P5 ✉ 111 Mason Street ☎ 800/771–1022 or 415/771–1200 🚌 38

HOTEL BOHEME $$

www.hotelboheme.com
Evoking 1950s North Beach, this cozy hotel with 15 small rooms plays up its connection to the literary Beat movement.
➕ P3 ✉ 444 Columbus Avenue ☎ 415/433–9111 🚌 30, 41, 45

A bay-view room, Mandarin Oriental

HOTEL DIVA $$

www.hoteldiva.com
Smack in the middle of the theater district, the Diva has 116 rooms with lots of chrome and other modern touches, though it can feel a bit sanitized.
➕ P5 ✉ 440 Geary Street ☎ 415/885–0200 or 800/553–1900 🚌 38

HOTEL DRISCO $$$

www.jdvhotels.com/drisco
Breakfast and evening wine are included in the cost of this 48-room hotel, built in 1903, in well-heeled Pacific Heights.
➕ K4 ✉ 2901 Pacific Avenue ☎ 800/634–7277 or 415/ 346–2880 🚌 3, 24

HOTEL FRANK $$–$$$

www.hotelfranksf.com
After an extensive redesign, the former Maxwell Hotel is now a popular 100-room boutique hotel with a retro esthetic and convenient Union Square location—at more reasonable prices than other hotels in the area.
➕ P5 ✉ 386 Geary Street ☎ 415/986–2000, 877/828–4478 🚌 38

HOTEL GRIFFON $$–$$$

www.hotelgriffon.com
This Embarcadero boutique hotel has 57 rooms and five suites, many with Bay Bridge views. Continental breakfast is included in the room price.
➕ R4 ✉ 155 Steuart Street ☎ 415/495–2100 or 800/321–2201 🚌 1, 14, 41

HOTEL MAJESTIC $$

www.thehotelmajestic.com
Formerly a private residence, this attractive hotel has 52 European-style rooms in Lower Pacific

Heights. Many rooms have claw-foot tubs and are decked out with antique furnishings.

➕ M5 ✉ 1500 Sutter Street ☎ 415/441–1100 or 800/869–8966 🚌 47, 49

HOTEL METROPOLIS $

www.hotelmetropolis.com

While its Tenderloin location is a bit dodgy, this 105-room hotel, decorated with bright colors, is about five blocks from Union Square and is also close to the theater district.

➕ P5 ✉ 25 Mason Street ☎ 415/775–4600 or 877/628–4412 🚌 Any Market Street bus; Powell-Hyde cable car

HOTEL REX $$

www.jdvhotels.com/rex

The lobby of this welcoming downtown hotel is filled with old books and the 94 rooms have a French country theme. There is live jazz on Friday nights in the lobby.

➕ P5 ✉ 562 Sutter Street ☎ 415/433–4434 or 800/433–4434 🚌 2, 3, 76

HOTEL DEL SOL $$

www.jdvhotels.com/del_sol

Bold, playful colors decorate this converted motor lodge in the Marina. The 57 rooms surround a pool.

➕ L3 ✉ 3100 Webster Street ☎ 415/921–5520 or 877/433–5765 🚌 22, 30

INN AT THE OPERA $$–$$$

www.shellhospitality.com/hotels/inn_at_the_opera

Quiet and elegant Inn at the Opera is a favorite of thespians and opera stars for its proximity to the performing-arts halls of Civic Center. There are 48 rooms.

➕ M6 ✉ 333 Fulton Street ☎ 800/325–2708 or 415/863–8400 🚌 5, 21

LAUREL INN $$

www.jdvhotels.com/laurel_inn

In a quiet part of town, this Laurel Heights lodge has 49 rooms, some with kitchenettes. It's near Sacramento Street shops.

➕ J5 ✉ 444 Presidio Avenue ☎ 415/567–8467 or 800/552–8735 🚌 1, 43

MANDARIN ORIENTAL $$$

www.mandarin-oriental.com/sanfrancisco

Mandarin Oriental is in the heart of the Financial District with 158 large, opulently furnished rooms; some rooms have city views.

➕ Q4 ✉ 222 Sansome Street ☎ 800/622–0404 or 415/276–9888 🚌 31, 38, 41

MARINA MOTEL $$

www.marinamotel.com

This plain and simple 39-room motel on the northern edge of Pacific Heights offers guests a choice of regular and kitchen-equipped rooms.

➕ K3 ✉ 2576 Lombard Street ☎ 800/346–6118 or 415/921–9406 🚌 28, 43, 76

THE PALACE HOTEL $$$

www.sfpalace.com

The city's first luxury hotel is located downtown. It's appropriate

SLEEP

Westin St. Francis, on Union Square

for royalty, heads of state and anyone with a taste for the finer things (553 rooms).

➕ Q5 ✉ 2 New Montgomery Street
☎ 800/325–3589 or 415/512–1111
🚇 Montgomery Street 🚌 5, 6, 9, 21, 31, 38, 45, 71

PHOENIX HOTEL $$
www.jdvhotels.com/phoenix
This self-proclaimed rocker hotel is in the tough Tenderloin neighborhood and close to popular music venues. It has 44 rooms, along with a courtyard pool and a new bar and lounge.

➕ N5 ✉ 601 Eddy Street ☎ 415/776–1380 or 800/248–9466 🚌 19, 31, 47

RED VICTORIAN BED, BREAKFAST & ART $$
www.redvic.com
The 18 themed guest rooms here include the Flower Child Room, the Skylight Room and the Summer of Love Room. It's in historic Haight-Ashbury, near to Golden Gate Park.

➕ J7 ✉ 1655 Haight Street ✉ 415/864–1978 🚌 6, 43, 71, N–Judah

RENOIR HOTEL $$
www.renoirhotel.com
A likeable flatiron-shape Civic Center landmark, the Renoir Hotel houses 133 simple but comfortable rooms. Be aware that the Market Street side can be noisy.

➕ P6 ✉ 45 McAllister Street
☎ 415/626–5200 or 800/576–3388
🚌 Any Market Street bus

RITZ-CARLTON SAN FRANCISCO $$$
www.ritzcarlton.com/sanfrancisco
After a $12.5 million renovation, this branch of the luxury chain is more grand than ever, with amenities like 400-thread-count sheets and stellar customer service. There are 336 rooms.

➕ P4 ✉ 600 Stockton Street
☎ 415/296–7465 or 800/241–3333
🚌 1, 2, 3, 30, 45, 91; Powell-Hyde cable car, California Street cable car

SAN REMO HOTEL $
www.sanremohotel.com
On the outskirts of North Beach, this 1906 Victorian building has

62 small rooms, although none has a private bathroom.

🔲 P2 ✉ 2237 Mason Street
☎ 415/776–8688 or 800/352–7366
🚌 9, 30

SLEEP OVER SAUCE $$

www.sleepsf.com

This 1906 Hayes Valley house is now an eight-room urban guest house. It sits above the restaurant Sauce, hence the name.

🔲 M7 ✉ 135 Gough Street ☎ 415/621–0896 🚌 21, Market Street buses

STANYAN PARK HOTEL $$

www.stanyanpark.com

Stanyan Park is a small (36 rooms), friendly hotel next to Golden Gate Park. Breakfast is included.

🔲 H8 ✉ 750 Stanyan Street
☎ 415/751–1000 🚌 6, 33, 43, 66, 71

TOWN HOUSE MOTEL $

www.sftownhousemotel.com

This 23-room motel is simply furnished, well kept and in a convenient Marina location. It serves a continental breakfast.

🔲 M3 ✉ 1650 Lombard Street
☎ 800/255–1516 or 415/885–5163 🚌 76

VILLAGE HOUSE $$

www.24henry.com

Choose from five tastefully themed rooms, from Asian to art deco, at this guest house in the Castro. You can also play the parlor piano.

🔲 L9 ✉ 4080 18th Street ☎ 800/900–5686 or 415/864–5686 🚌 33

WASHINGTON SQUARE INN $$$

www.wsisf.com

This boutique hotel has prime real estate on this lovely North Beach square. A few of the 15 rooms have views of Coit Tower.

🔲 P3 ✉ 1660 Stockton Street
☎ 415/981–4220 or 800/388–0220
🚌 30, 41, 45

WESTIN ST. FRANCIS $$$

www.westinstfrancis.com

Westin St. Francis has been a San Franciscan landmark since 1904 and is resoundingly aristocratic. There are nearly 1,200 rooms.

🔲 P5 ✉ 335 Powell Street at Union Square ☎ 800/WESTIN 1 or 415/397–7000 🚌 2, 3, 6, 38, 71; Powell–Hyde or Powell–Mason cable car

WHITE SWAN INN $$$

www.jdvhotels.com/white_swan_inn

A breakfast buffet and complimentary evening wine add to the already rich atmosphere of this Nob Hill 26-room, antique-decorated inn.

🔲 P4 ✉ 845 Bush Street ☎ 800/999–9570 or 415/ 775–1755 🚌 2, 3, 76

WILLOWS INN $

www.willowssf.com

This gay-friendly Castro inn has 12 rooms, each with a washbasin, and shared bathrooms down the hall. Continental breakfast is included.

🔲 L8 ✉ 710 14th Street ☎ 415/431–4770 or 800/431–0277 🚌 Any Market Street bus

W HOTEL $$$

www.starwoodhotels.com

A modern SoMa property close to the San Francisco Museum of Modern Art and downtown, this hotel has 404 rooms, a lap pool, Bliss Spa and the lively XYZ Bar.

🔲 Q5 ✉ 181 3rd Street ☎ 415/777–5300 or 877/946–8357 🚌 14, 30, 45

Need to Know

This section takes you through all the practical aspects of your trip to make it run more smoothly and to give you confidence before you go and while you are there.

Planning Ahead

WHEN TO GO

San Francisco's peak tourist months are July and August and hotels are busy. September and October are better times to visit, as the crowds have thinned and the weather is warm and sunny. Take a sweater and jacket for evening as fogs off the Pacific Ocean can chill the air.

TIME

San Francisco is on Pacific Time, eight hours behind the UK and nine hours behind Western Europe.

TEMPERATURE

JAN	FEB	MAR	APR	MAY	JUN	JUL	AUG	SEP	OCT	NOV	DEC
55°F	54°F	55°F	55°F	61°F	61°F	61°F	61°F	70°F	70°F	61°F	54°F
13°C	12°C	13°C	13°C	16°C	16°C	16°C	16°C	21°C	21°C	16°C	12°C

Spring (March to May) fogs usually occur only in the morning and have lifted by midday as the temperature rises.

Summer (June to August) weather is unpredictable. One day may be warm and sunny and the next a chilly fog appears in the morning and lingers through the evening.

Fall (September to November) sees the warmest and clearest days of the year.

Winter (December to February) rain can be heavy, especially in January. There are often torrential storms and it can rain for several days. Most rainfall occurs during winter.

WHAT'S ON

January/February *Chinese New Year*: Two weeks of Chinatown festivities; date depends on lunar cycle.

March *St. Patrick's Day* (Mar 17): Irish and would-be-Irish dress in green for a parade on Market Street.

April *Cherry Blossom Festival*: Japantown celebrates Japanese art and culture.

May *Cinco de Mayo* (May 5): Mexican celebration centered in the Mission District.

Bay to Breakers: Athletes and exhibitionists race from one side of the city to the other.

Carnaval: The Mission District fills with music, floats and costumes.

June *Gay Pride Parade*: Huge march, usually starting or ending at Civic Center Plaza.

North Beach Festival: Music, food and sidewalk chalk art.

July *Independence Day* (Jul 4): Fireworks and a 50-cannon salute on the northern waterfront.

San Francisco Marathon: The country's third-largest marathon crosses Golden Gate Bridge.

August *Outside Lands Music and Arts Festival*: A multi-day festival in Golden Gate Park.

September *Shakespeare in the Park*: Free outdoor performances in the Presidio. Each summer features a different play by the Bard.

October *Fleet Week*: The US Navy's Blue Angels do a popular and daring air show, and they fly under the Golden Gate Bridge.

November *Day of the Dead* (Nov 2): Mexican tribute to the spirit world, with a parade through the Mission District.

December *Tchaikovsky's Nutcracker*: In a winter tradition, the San Francisco Ballet performs at the War Memorial Opera House.

SAN FRANCISCO ONLINE

San Francisco has excellent websites with regularly updated information on everything from the theater to news, weather and gossip.

www.citysbest.com/sanfrancisco
www.sanfrancisco.citysearch.com
Professional reviews with local tips covering shops, restaurants, nightspots, museums, cinemas, theaters and more.

www.sfstation.com
Cutting-edge nightclubs, bars and stores.

www.theatrebayarea.org
Theater news and listings.

www.nps.gov
Factual information on the city's federally run parks, including Alcatraz.

www.diggers.org
Tells the story of the proto-hippie Diggers, active in Haight-Ashbury in the mid-1960s and full of radical ideas even today.

www.sfgate.com
The *San Francisco Chronicle* website, with dining, nightlife and events news.

www.sfbg.com
www.sfweekly.com
The influential websites of the free papers *San Francisco Bay Guardian* and *SF Weekly*.

www.sanfran.com
San Francisco magazine dispenses ideas for elegant shopping, dining and generally spending money around town.

www.511.org
Brings Bay Area travel, be it by car, bike, bus, train or plane, into a single site.

www.flavorpill.com/sanfrancisco
A guide to events in the city, from quirky to mainstream.

PRIME TRAVEL SITES

www.bart.gov
www.sfmta.com
Timetables, routes and fares.
www.ci.sf.ca.us
The city's administration provides more practical information.
www.fodors.com
A travel-planning site where you can research prices and weather, book tickets, cars and rooms and ask fellow travelers questions; links to other sites.

INTERNET CAFÉS

Most hotels and many cafés and bars in San Francisco offer free or low-cost internet access, including the Starbucks and Coffee Bean & Tea Leaf chains. The following stand out in this fully wired city:

● Gallery Café (✉ 1200 Mason Street ☎ 415/296–9932) has organic breads, gourmet coffee and free internet access.
● MaggieMudd (✉ 903 Cortland Avenue ☎ 415/641–5291) allows you to use free access as the excuse for sampling the dozens of flavors of ice cream here.
● Quetzal (✉ 1234 Polk Street ☎ 415/673–4181) sells green coffees and a range of fruit smoothies.

Getting There

ENTRY REQUIREMENTS

Visitors from outside the US must show a passport valid for at least six months. You must have a return or onward ticket. Visitors from the UK who are eligible for the Visa Waiver Program, and eligible visitors from other countries with visa waiver status, must register with the US's Electronic System for Travel Authorization (ESTA™). Register online at https://esta.cbp.dhs.gov/esta at least 72 hours prior to travel, preferably much earlier. This is valid for stays of 90 days or less. For further details, or for visa information for longer stays, go online at www.usembassy.org.uk. Always check the latest entry requirements before traveling. Note that due to heightened security measures, it may take longer to pass through security checkpoints at the airport.

CULTURE AT SFO

In the International Terminal you'll find the San Francisco Airport Commission Aviation Library and Louis A. Turpen Aviation Museum, which chronicles the history of aviation through photographs and objects. In addition, the San Francisco Arts Commission selects the permanent art—including paintings, sculptures and mosaics—that is displayed throughout the airport.

AIRPORTS

There are direct flights to San Francisco from all over the world. The main airport is San Francisco International (SFO). You can also fly into Oakland International Airport and San Jose International.

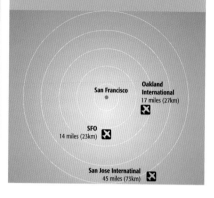

San Francisco

Oakland International
17 miles (27km)

SFO
14 miles (23km)

San Jose Internatinal
45 miles (73km)

FROM SFO

San Francisco International Airport (tel 650/821–8211; www.flysfo.com) is 14 miles (23km) south of the city. BART (tel 415/989–2278) runs directly to the city from the airport, cost $8.10, and takes around 30 minutes. Airport Express Coaches (tel 415/775–5121) take visitors from the airport to the city every 30 minutes between 4.30am and 10pm, cost $18 one way, and take an hour to make the journey. Privately run minibuses such as SuperShuttle (tel 650/558–8500) pick up from the traffic island outside and cost approximately $17 per person. A taxi into the city costs $40–$50.

FROM OAKLAND INTERNATIONAL

Oakland International Airport (tel 510/563–3300; www.flyoakland.com), which serves both domestic and international flights, is across the Bay, 17 miles (27km) from San Francisco. You travel into the city via I-880 and I-80; traffic on the Bay Bridge may make travel time longer. A taxi will get you to the city in about 35–45 minutes, costing around $50 one way, depending on your destination. Otherwise take the Air-BART shuttle to the

Coliseum/Oakland station, cost $3, and catch the next BART to the city; cost is around $3.80.

FROM SAN JOSE INTERNATIONAL

The city's third airport (tel 408/277–4759; www.sjc.org), although about 45 miles (73km) south of downtown San Francisco, is well served by domestic carriers. Take the VTA Airport Flyer (route 10) to Santa Clara station and then CalTrain (tel 800/660–4287) to the city, which takes about 80 minutes and costs $8.50.

MORE AIRPORT INFORMATION

Airport websites have a plethora of useful information, including the list of airlines that serve the airport, ground transportation, driving directions, maps and security status. Oakland's site even provides real-time weather and traffic reports. For up-to-date security information and precautions from the US Transportation Security Administration, check out the agency's comprehensive web-site www.tsa.gov and click on "For Travelers."

TEMPORARY TRANSBAY TERMINAL

San Francisco's Transbay Terminal at First and Mission streets is undergoing a massive $4.2 billion transformation. The new Transbay Transit Center will be a 1 million sq ft (93,000sq m) hub and landmark, with a 5.4-acre (2.2ha) public park on its roof. Until the new terminal opens in the summer of 2017, the Transbay Temporary Terminal (tel 415/977–0531; www.temporaryterminal.org) is located at Howard and Main streets.

ARRIVING BY BUS

Greyhound buses (tel 800/229–9424) into the city terminate at the Transbay Temporary Terminal (▷ above).

ARRIVING BY TRAIN

Amtrak (tel 800/872–7245; www.amtrak.com) serves Emeryville east of the city, and provides free shuttle buses from there to various stops in San Francisco.

INSURANCE

Traveler's insurance is strongly recommended. Keep in mind that there are two different types: Trip insurance can minimize your losses in the event that you have to cancel or delay a trip, while medical travel insurance protects you if you incur medical expenses while traveling (▷ 169). Check your current policy and buy supplementary cover if necessary.

VISITORS WITH DISABILITIES

Aside from its steep hills, San Francisco is generally a good city for visitors using a wheelchair, with ramped public buildings and accessible buses, BART stations and taxis. Some hotels have roll-in showers, and some have Braille signage. For details, see *Access San Francisco*, a free annually updated booklet published by Access Northern California (www.accessnca.com), available from the Convention & Visitors Bureau. Also contact the Mayor's Office on Disability ✉ 401 Van Ness Avenue, Room 300, San Francisco, CA 94102 ☎ 415/554–6789; www.ci.sf.ca.us/sfmod

Getting Around

DRIVING

- Unless posted higher, the limit is 25mph (40kph) in school zones, business and residential areas.
- Maximum speed on freeways is 65mph (105kph), 70mph (113kph) where specifically posted, except on downtown freeways, where it is 55mph (89kph), and on construction zones.
- A right turn on a red light after stopping is legal unless posted otherwise, as is a left on red at the intersection of two one-way streets.
- There is a toll for drivers coming south across the Golden Gate Bridge, and west across the Bay Bridge.
- If you belong to a motoring organization, check its links with the AAA California State Automobile Association, which offers free maps to members ⊠ 160 Sutter Street ☎ 415/773–1900.

Much of San Francisco can be explored on foot but the city has an excellent system of buses and cable cars, as well as the underground BART system, which is chiefly used for crossing the bay to Berkeley and Oakland. MUNI buses and metro trains (tel 415/673–MUNI) serve the outer neighborhoods. Use taxis if you are in a rush, traveling late at night or want to pass quickly through edgy neighborhoods. A MUNI Passport (www.sfmta.com/cms/mfares/passports.htm), which is valid on MUNI buses, streetcars and cable cars for one, three or seven days costs $14, $21 or $27 respectively. Muni Passports can be bought at the Visitor Information Center (▷ 170).

BART

Fares range from $1.75 to $10.55 according to distance traveled. Tickets can be bought from machines at BART stations. Operating times are Mon–Fri 4am–midnight, Sat 6am–midnight, Sun 8am–midnight. All BART stations display maps of the BART system. For further information tel 415/989–2278.

BIKING

Despite the hilly terrain, biking is a popular way to get around in San Francisco and avoid the hassles of parking. Rentals are available all over the city, including Blazing Saddles (1095 Columbus Avenue and Pier 41, among other locations; tel 415/202–8888); and Bay City Bike (2661 Taylor Street, 501 Bay Street and 1325 Columbus Avenue; tel 415/346–2453).

BUSES

Buses cover the entire city, operating 5am–1am; outside these hours Owl Service buses provide a reduced-frequency service on main routes. The flat fare is currently $2; to change buses on a single ride, ask the driver for a free transfer ticket. Exact change is necessary and should be fed into the machine next to the driver when boarding. Bus routes are shown in the phone book and at most bus stops. Maps and timetables are available from City Hall and, in a style more accessible for visitors (and including BART routes), from the Visitor Center Hallidie Plaza.

CABLE CARS

Cable cars, more a tourist attraction than a practical means of getting around, operate on three routes between 6.30am and 12.30am: Powell–Mason and Powell–Hyde run between Market Street and Fisherman's Wharf, and California Street runs between the Financial District and Nob Hill. Tickets cost $5 per ride and can be bought from the self-service machines at the end of each route, or from the conductor when you board.

CAR RENTAL

● All international car-rental companies have desks at SFO, as well as offices in the city.
● Alamo: SFO, tel 800/462–5266
● Avis: SFO, tel 800/230–4898
● Budget Rent-a-Car: SFO, tel 800/527–0700
● Dollar: SFO, tel 800/800–4000
● Dubbelju (motorcycles), tel 415/495–2774
● Hertz: SFO, tel 800/654–3131
● Seatbelts are compulsory for all passengers and the driver. Child restraints are mandatory for under six-year-olds or children weighing less than 60lb (27kg).
● On-the-spot fines can be imposed for speeding, with the level of fine depending on the amount over the limit. Over 25mph (40kph), you may have to go to court.

TAXIS

Taxis can be hailed in the street or from taxi stands at major hotels and at transportation terminals. During rush hours (7–9am and 4–6pm) and rain, it is hard to find a free taxi cruising the streets. Average taxi fares are $3.10 for pick up and 45¢ per every fifth of a mile. Hotel receptionists can order a taxi for you on request, or you can phone one of the following firms:
De Soto, tel 415/970–1300
Fog City, tel 415/285–3800
Luxor, tel 415/282–4141
Yellow, tel 415/333–3333

PARKING

Parking restrictions are enforced with vigor. The city has many off-street and multistory parking lots, in addition to meters, many of which now take credit cards. When parking on the city's steep hills, you are required by law to turn downhill-facing vehicles' front wheels into the curb; uphill-facing vehicles should have their wheels turned to the street.

CITY PASS

San Francisco offers visitors the City Pass, which is a booklet of tickets for sights in the city. It costs $69 ($39 for kids) and includes admission for six attractions and a seven-day MUNI and Cable Car Passport. Sights include SFMOMA, the California Academy of Sciences and the Exploratorium.

Essential Facts

Nearly all banks have Automatic Teller Machines (ATMs). Credit cards are widely accepted. A 9.5 percent sales tax is added to marked retail prices. Funds can be wired via: American Express MoneyGram ☎ 800/926–9400 for US and Canada locations; Western Union ☎ 800/325–6000 for agent locations (or to send using MasterCard or Visa).

EMBASSIES

● Germany ✉ 1960 Jackson Street ☎ 415/775–1061
● Ireland ✉ 100 Pine Street ☎ 415/392–4214
● Italy ✉ 2590 Webster Street ☎ 415/292–9200
● Japan ✉ 50 Fremont Street ☎ 415/777–3533
● Mexico ✉ 532 Folsom Street ☎ 415/354–1700
● Spain ✉ 1405 Sutter Street ☎ 415/922–2995
● UK ✉ 1 Sansome Street, Suite 850 ☎ 415/617–1300

CURRENCY
The unit of currency is the dollar (=100 cents). Notes (bills) come in denominations of $1, $5, $10, $20, $50 and $100; coins are 25¢ (a quarter), 10¢ (a dime), 5¢ (a nickel) and 1¢ (a penny).

ELECTRICITY
The supply is 100 volts, 60 cycles AC current. US appliances use two-prong plugs. European appliances require an adapter.

EMERGENCY PHONE NUMBERS
● Fire, police or ambulance: 911
● Rape Crisis Hotline: 415/647–7273
● Victims of Crime Resource Center: 800/842–8467

LAVATORIES
Public buildings are obliged to provide lavatories, which are almost always well maintained, as are those in hotel lobbies, restaurants and most bars.

LOST PROPERTY PHONE NUMBERS
● San Francisco International Airport: 650/821–7014
● Amtrak station in Oakland: 800/872–7245
● MUNI buses or cable cars: 311

MEDICINES
Pharmacies are plentiful and details can be found online or in the Yellow Pages listed under "Drugstores." Visitors from Europe will find many familiar medicines are sold under unfamiliar names. Note that some medication bought over the counter at home might be prescription-only in the US and may be confiscated at customs if you don't have a doctor's certificate for essential medication.

NEWSPAPERS AND MAGAZINES
San Francisco has two daily newspapers, the *San Francisco Chronicle* and the free *San Francisco Examiner*, and two free weekly papers, *SF Weekly* and *San Francisco Bay*

Guardian. Free tourist-aimed magazines are found in hotel lobbies; their discount coupons can save money on sightseeing and food.

OPENING HOURS

● Stores open daily, usually from around 10–6. Department stores, chain stores and shopping malls often have longer hours, while boutiques sometimes close on Sundays.
● Banks open Mon–Fri 9–4, 5 or 6; some branches open Saturday.
● Post offices usually open Mon–Fri 9–5.30, with limited hours on Saturday.

PLACES OF WORSHIP

Hotel receptions can advise and the phone book carries a comprehensive list.

POST SERVICES

● Stamps are available from post offices and also at some hotel receptions, vending machines and ATMs.
● Find the nearest post office by looking in the phone book or online or asking at your hotel.

PUBLIC HOLIDAYS

● Jan 1: New Year's Day
● Third Mon in Jan: Martin Luther King Day
● Third Mon in Feb: President's Day
● Last Mon in May: Memorial Day
● Jul 4: Independence Day
● First Mon in Sep: Labor Day
● Second Mon in Oct: Columbus Day
● Nov 11: Veterans' Day
● Fourth Thu in Nov: Thanksgiving Day
● Dec 25: Christmas Day

SENSIBLE PRECAUTIONS

San Francisco is one of the country's safest cities and lone travelers, especially women, are not unusual. Unwelcome attention is not unknown, and areas such as the Tenderloin, parts of the Mission, Oakland, the Haight, Golden Gate Park, Western Addition and the outskirts of the city, may seem threatening

ETIQUETTE

● Be aware of the anti-smoking feeling that prevails in San Francisco. Smoking is illegal in bars, restaurants and nightclubs throughout California.
● Tip at least 15 percent in a restaurant; 15–20 percent of a taxi fare; $1 per bag to a porter.

MEDICAL TREATMENT

● Doctor referral: San Francisco Medical Society
☎ 415/561-0850
● Dentist: San Francisco Dental Society
☎ 415/928-7337
● City hospitals with 24-hour emergency rooms:
San Francisco General
✉ 1001 Potrero Avenue
☎ 415/206-8000;
Davies Medical Center
✉ Castro Street (at Duboce Street) ☎ 415/600-6000
● Medicines: 24-hour pharmacy Walgreens offers a service at:
✉ 3201 Divisadero Street
☎ 415/931-6417;
✉ 498 Castro Street
☎ 415/861-3136
● It is strongly recommended to take out comprehensive medical insurance before traveling.

after dark. Do not carry easily snatched bags and cameras, or stuff your wallet into your back pocket. Always keep your belongings within sight and within reach. Keep valuables in the hotel's safe and never carry more cash than you need. If you plan to make an insurance claim, report any item stolen to the nearest police precinct as soon as possible. It is unlikely that any stolen goods will be recovered, but the police will fill out the forms that your insurance company will need.

TELEPHONES

● Thanks to the popularity of cell phones, public telephones are now difficult to find, although they can still sometimes be found in the street, hotel lobbies, restaurants and public buildings.
● Many businesses have toll-free numbers, prefixed 800, 866, 877 or 888, allowing the public to phone them for free. First dial "1."
● Most US phones use touch-tone dialing; each button issues a different electronic tone as it is pressed, enabling the caller to access extensions directly, following the instructions given by a recorded voice.
● The area code for San Francisco is 415, which should not be dialed if calling from another 415 number. The code for Berkeley and Oakland is 510, and San Jose is 408.
● To call the operator dial "0."
● Dial 311 to reach the San Francisco customer service line. You can call 24 hours a day with questions about government-related services—or even to report a pothole.

TELEVISION AND RADIO

● Linked to national networks, the main San Francisco TV channels are 2, KTVU (FOX); 3, KNTV (NBC); 5, KPIX (CBS); 7, KGO (ABC); and the public-run 9, KQED (PBS). These give the usual range of programs plus local and national news.
● San Francisco has some 80 radio stations. Generally, the best talk and news shows are on the AM waveband, while the best music is on FM stations.

Films and Books

FILMS

Vertigo (1958): This Hitchcock masterpiece stars Jimmy Stewart as an acrophobic San Francisco detective and Kim Novak as the woman he becomes obsessed with. SF locations include Lombard Street, the Legion of Honor and Nob Hill.

The Graduate (1967): The coming-of-age drama features Dustin Hoffman as a recent college graduate and Anne Bancroft as Mrs. Robinson, the sexy older woman who seduces him.

Bullitt (1968): Lieutenant Frank Bullitt (Steve McQueen) must protect a Chicago mob boss turned government witness, but Bullitt soon discovers he doesn't have all the facts. The car chase through San Francisco is famous.

Dirty Harry (1971): Inspector Harry Callahan (Clint Eastwood) must stop a lunatic from terrorizing San Francisco. Locations include 555 California Street, City Hall, Mission Dolores Park and Washington Square.

Escape from Alcatraz (1979): This movie, based on a true story, focuses on a group of convicts (including one played by Clint Eastwood) who try to escape from Alcatraz.

Mrs. Doubtfire (1993): Robin Williams disguises himself as a nanny to spend time with his children after an ugly divorce. His new employer/ex-wife lives at 2640 Steiner Street.

The Rock (1996): This Michael Bay thriller features Nicolas Cage and Sean Connery as the good guys trying to stop a crazy general from launching warheads into San Francisco.

The Game (1997): Michael Douglas is a financier who receives an unusual birthday gift from his brother (Sean Penn). Watch for 555 California, the Embarcadero and the Presidio.

The Pursuit of Happyness (2006): This is based on Chris Gardner's true story about a man (played by Will Smith) who loses everything, but fights for survival and success. It shows Candlestick Park and Golden Gate Park.

Milk (2008): Sean Penn stars as politician and gay-rights activist Harvey Milk, the first openly gay elected official in California. The film was shot in locations all over San Francisco.

BOOKS

● *The Maltese Falcon* by Dashiell Hammett (1930): Hammett's influential detective novel was adapted into one of the first movies of the film noir genre, with Humphrey Bogart as private investigator Sam Spade.

● *On the Road* by Jack Kerouac (1951): The Bible of the Beat Generation, part of this semi-autobiographical road-trip novel takes place in San Francisco, which figured prominently in the Beat movement.

● *Tales of the City* by Armistead Maupin (1978): What started as a newspaper serial morphed into a series of books about the escapades of Mary Ann Singleton, a woman who moves to San Francisco from Ohio.

● *The Joy Luck Club* by Amy Tan (1989): Mothers and daughters from four Chinese-American immigrant families start a mahjong club and share their stories.

● *Daughter of Fortune* by Isabel Allende (1999): Part 2 of this Oprah Book Club selection takes the protagonist to the City by the Bay.

Index

The Automobile Association would like to thank the following photographers and companies for their assistance in the preparation of this book.

Abbreviations for the picture credits are as follows: (t) top; (b) bottom; (l) left; (r) right; (c) center (AA) AA World Travel Library.

2i, 2iii, 2v AA/C Sawyer; **2ii** AA/K Paterson; **2iv** Chris Howes/Wild Places Photography/Alamy; **3i** Bill Helsel/Alamy; **3ii** AA/C Sawyer; **3iii** Mandarin Oriental, San Francisco; **3iv–6/7ct** AA/C Sawyer; **6cb, 7ct** Lee Foster/Alamy; **7cb** Photodisc; **6/7b** Keystone USA-ZUMA/Rex Features; **8tr** AA/C Sawyer; **9tl** Chris Howes/Wild Places Photography/Alamy; **8/9c** AA/K Paterson; **9ct** Travel Division Images/Alamy; **9cb** Cobb's Comedy Club; **8/9b** AA/C Sawyer; **10l, 10r** AA/K Paterson; **11** AA/C Sawyer; **12** AA/K Paterson; **14l** David R. Frazier Photolibrary, Inc./Alamy; **14/15t, 14/15c, 15** AA/C Sawyer; **16, 17tl** Paul Vidler/Alamy; **17cl** AA/K Paterson; **17r** Photolibrary; **18–19cr** © Tim Griffith; **19tr** Charles Delbeek; **20–21** Chinese Historical Society of America; **22, 23tl** AA/C Sawyer; **23cl** Miguel A. Munoz Pellicer/Alamy; **23r** Frank Tozier/Alamy; **24** AA/C Sawyer; **25tl** AA/K Paterson; **25tr** Lee Foster/Alamy; **25c** David R. Frazier Photolibrary, Inc./Alamy; **26, 27r** The Neptune Society of Northern California; **27tl** AA/C Sawyer; **27cl** Robert Holmes/Corbis; **28l** Monica M. Davey/epa/Corbis; **28/9t, 28/9c** Art on File/Corbis; **29r** Architec Tour/Alamy; **30–31** Fine Arts Museums of San Francisco; **32/33t, 33cr** Amy Snyder © Exploratorium, All rights reserved; **32/33c** Nancy Rodger © Exploratorium, All rights reserved; **33tr** Lily Rodriguez © Exploratorium, All rights reserved **34, 34/35c, 35tr** AA/C Sawyer; **35cr** John Gilbey/Alamy; **36** AA/K Paterson; **36/37–39tl** AA/C Sawyer; **39c** AA/L K Stow; **40–41cr** AA/C Sawyer; **41cl** AA/K Paterson; **42l, 42/43t** Neil Setchfield/Alamy; **42/43c** Jon Arnold Images Ltd/Alamy; **43tr** AA/K Paterson; **43cr** AA/C Sawyer; **44** Craig Lovell/Eagle Visions Photography/Alamy; **45tl, 45tr** AA/K Paterson; **45c–47** AA/C Sawyer; **48t, 49l, 49tr** Photograph by Steve Whittaker © FAMSF; **48c** AA/C Sawyer; **49cr** Fine Arts Museums of San Francisco; **50l, 50/1** AA/K Paterson; **51tr** dbimages/Alamy; **51cl** dk/Alamy; **52–53c** Oakland Museum of California; **53tr** Tim Griffith/Oakland Museum of California; **54l** AA/K Paterson; **54r** San Francisco/Alamy; **55tr** Aerial Archives/Alamy; **55cr** Dennis Hallinan/Alamy; **56l** Craig Lovell/Eagle Visions Photography/Alamy; **56/57** Craig Lovell/Eagle Visions Photography/Alamy; **57tr** Photo: Richard Barnes/San Francisco Museum of Modern Art; **57cr** Ryan K. McGinnis/Alamy; **58/59** AA/C Sawyer; **59** Neil Fraser/Alamy; **60l** Courtesy UC Berkeley; **60/61–61r** Steve McConnell/UC Berkeley; **62–64** AA/C Sawyer; **66** Photos by Kaz Tsuruta/Asian Art Museum; **67–68** AA/C Sawyer; **69l** david sanger photography/Alamy; **69r–72** AA/C Sawyer; **73l** Nikreates/Alamy; **73r** AA/C Sawyer; **75l** Lee Foster/Alamy; **75r** AA/K Paterson; **76** Ambient Images Inc./Alamy; **77** Chad Ehlers/Alamy; **78–79** AA/C Sawyer; **80** Chris Howes/Wild Places Photography/Alamy; **82tr** Dave Pattison/Alamy; **82bl** Rubens Abboud/Alamy; **83t** AA/C Sawyer; **83c** Photo by Cesar Rubio, Courtesy The Walt Disney Family Museum; **83b** Dennis MacDonald/Alamy; **86i** Amy Snyder © Exploratorium, All rights reserved; **86ii, 86iii** AA/C Sawyer; **86iv** Photograph by Steve Whittaker © FAMSF; **86v** Dennis Hallinan/Alamy; **87–92c** AA/C Sawyer; **92b** AA/K Paterson; **94** AA/C Sawyer; **95t** AA/K Paterson; **95b** AA/C Sawyer; **98l** AA/K Paterson; **98r–101c** AA/C Sawyer; **101b** dbimages/Alamy; **104t, 104c** AA/C Sawyer; **104b** AA/K Paterson; **106t** AA/C Sawyer; **106b** Fine Arts Museums of San Francisco; **107** AA/C Sawyer; **110i** © Tim Griffith; **110ii** The Neptune Society of Northern California; **110iii** Fine Arts Musuems of San Francisco; **110iv** AA/K Paterson; **111** AA/C Sawyer; **112t** Steve McConnell/UC Berkeley; **112b** Oakland Museum of California; **113t** Lee Foster/Alamy; **113l** AA/C Sawyer; **116t** Oakland Museum of California; **116b** Steve McConnell/UC Berkeley; **117** Bonnie Azab Powell/UC Berkeley; **118–127** AA/C Sawyer; **128** Bill Helsel/Alamy; **130/131t** AA/C Sawyer; **130/131c** Emmanuel Rondeau/Alamy; **131ct** AA/Yadid Levy; **131cb** AA/A Mockford & N Bonetti; **130/131b** Arco Images GmbH/Alamy; **137** Werner Dieterich/Alamy; **138** AA/C Sawyer; **140t** Photodisc; **140ct–140b** AA/C Sawyer; **142–147l** Photodisc; **147r** AA/T Carter; **148l** Photodisc; **148r** AA/J Tims; **150** Mandarin Oriental, San Francisco; **152t** AA/A Mockford & N Bonetti; **152ct** AA/K Paterson; **152cb** AA/M Bonnet; **152b** AA/J Tims; **156** Mandarin Oriental, San Francisco; **158** Lee Foster/Alamy; **160** AA/C Sawyer.

Every effort has been made to trace the copyright holders, and we apologise in advance for any unintentional omissions or errors. We would be pleased to apply any corrections in a following edition of this publication.

San Francisco's 25 Best

WRITTEN BY Mick Sinclair
ADDITIONAL WRITING BY Julie Jares
SERIES EDITOR Marie-Claire Jefferies
REVIEWING EDITOR Linda Schmidt
PROJECT EDITOR Kathryn Glendenning
COVER DESIGN Guido Caroti
DESIGN WORK Catherine Murray
INDEXER Marie Lorimer
PICTURE RESEARCHER Carol Walker
IMAGE RETOUCHING AND REPRO Jacqueline Street

ISBN 978-1-4000-0399-0

EIGHTH EDITION

IMPORTANT TIP
Time inevitably brings changes, so always confirm prices, travel facts, and other perishable information when it matters. Although Fodor's cannot accept responsibility for errors, you can use this guide in the confidence that we have taken every care to ensure its accuracy.

SPECIAL SALES
This book is available for special discounts for bulk purchases for sales promotions or premiums. Special editions, including personalized covers, excerpts of existing books, and corporate imprints, can be created in large quantities for special needs. For more information, write to Special Markets/Premium Sales, 1745 Broadway, 3-2, New York, NY 10019 or email specialmarkets@randomhouse.com.

Color separation by AA Digital Department
Printed and bound by Leo Paper Products, China

10 9 8 7 6 5 4 3 2

Cover image: Stas Volik/Shutterstock

A04966
Maps in this title produced from map data supplied by Global Mapping, Brackley, UK © Global Mapping/ITMB
Transport map © Communicarta Ltd, UK

Titles in the Series